1978

CHILTON'S

Auto Troubleshooting Guide ILLUSTRATED

Prepared by the

Automotive Editorial Department

Chilton Book Company
Chilton Way
Radnor, Pa. 19089
215–687-8200

president and chief executive officer **WILLIAM A. BARBOUR;** executive vice president **RICHARD H. GROVES;** vice president and general manager **WILLIAM D. BYRNE;** associate editorial director **GLEN B. RUH;** managing editor **JOHN H. WEISE, S.A.E.;** assistant managing editor **STEPHEN J. DAVIS;** editor **John M. Baxter**

CHILTON BOOK COMPANY   RADNOR, PENNSYLVANIA

7890   210987

Library of Congress Cataloging in Publication Data

Chilton Book Company.   Automotive Editorial Department.
   Chilton's auto troubleshooting guide.

   1. Automobiles—Maintenance and repair.   I. Title.
TL152.C5226   629.28'8   73-4259
ISBN 0-8019-5745-1 pbk.
ISBN 0-8019-6080-0

ACKNOWLEDGMENTS

Chilton Book Company expresses appreciation to the following
individual and his firm for their generous assistance:

William A. Baxter
FIRESTONE TIRE AND RUBBER COMPANY

Contents

Intr

While adequate automotive repairs can be performed by many persons, both professional and non-professional, troubleshooting seems to be a very rare skill. The garageman *and* car owner can save time, money, and trouble if they approach automotive problems with a basic knowledge of troubleshooting. It is the purpose of this volume to make that knowledge available in an easily understood form.

Each chapter or section begins with a description of the basic operating principles of the system it deals with. Also, Chapter 10, The Electrical System, begins with a description of basic electrical theory. We suggest that these portions of the text be given a careful reading, even if the reading will only serve as a review. The most important key to effective diagnosis is complete understanding.

Note also that Chapters One through Four and the Charging System section of Chapter 9 contain quick reference guides to troubleshooting procedures. These will streamline troubleshooting for those who are familiar with the basic test procedures.

Introduction

1 · The Basics of Engine Operation

Cross section of a typical V8 engine (© Ford Motor Co)

The modern automobile engine is certainly the most complex and highly stressed of all household machines. Its parts are subjected to higher temperatures, greater pressures and vibration, and more extreme frictional loads and changes in velocity than those of other common machines. It has also been developed and refined to a greater extent than most machines. As a result, while the basic operating principles are fairly simple, the specifics are quite complex, and even the smallest deviation from the norm in the dimensions or the condition of a part, or in the setting of an individual adjustment can result in an obvious operating defect.

This first section is designed to relate engine operating principles to the most

1

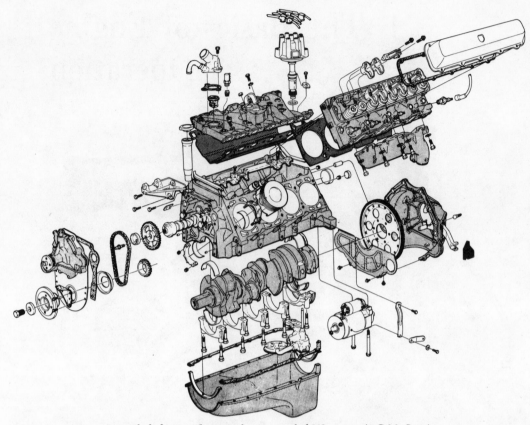

An exploded view of a typical water-cooled V8 engine (© G.M. Corp)

common malfunctions so that the troubleshooter may visualize the physical relationship between the two. While it will be a review for many, it should help to provide the type of understanding that will enable the reader to replace time-consuming guesswork with quick, efficient troubleshooting.

The engine is a metal block containing a series of chambers. The volume of these chambers varies in relation to the position

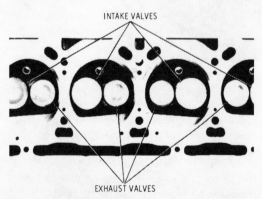

The combustion chamber in a typical V8 cylinder head (© G.M. Corp)

of a rotating shaft. There is a port for each chamber which provides for the admission of combustible material and another port for the expulsion of burned gases. The combustion chambers' volumes must be variable in order for the engine to be able to make use of the expansion of the burning gases. This ability also enables the chamber to compress the gases before combustion, and to purge itself of burned material and refill itself with a combustible charge after combustion has taken place. (A description of how these four functions are accomplished follows the material on basic engine construction.)

The upper engine block is usually an iron or aluminum alloy casting, consisting of outer walls which form hollow water jackets around the four, six, or eight cylinder walls. The lower block provides an appropriate number of rigid mounting points for the bearings which hold the crankshaft in place, and is known as the crankcase. The hollow jackets of the upper block add to the rigidity of the structure and contain the liquid coolant which carries the heat away from the cylinders and other parts of

A typical V8 cylinder block, bottom view (© G.M. Corp)

TIMING MARKS

THRUST PLATE SCREWS

The block provides mounting points for the engine's camshaft and its drive mechanism (© G.M. Corp)

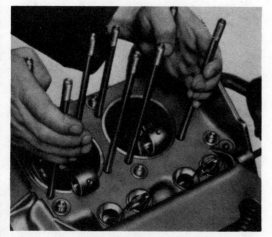

The crankcase of an air cooled engine (© Volkswagon of America, Inc)

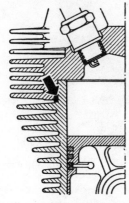

Cross-section of an air-cooled cylinder showing the cooling fins on the cylinder (© Volkswagon of America, Inc)

the block. The block of an air-cooled engine consists of a crankcase which provides for the rigid mounting of the crankshaft and for the studs which hold the cylinders rigidly in place. The cylinders are usually individual, single-wall castings, and are finned for cooling.

The block (both air-cooled and water-cooled) also provides rigid mounts for the engine's camshaft and its drive gears or drive chain. In water-cooled engines, studs are installed in the top of the block to provide for the rigid mounting of the cylinder heads on to the top of the block. The water and oil pumps are usually mounted directly to the block.

The crankshaft is a long iron alloy or steel fabrication which consists of bearing points or journals, which turn on their own axes, and counterweighted crank throws or crankpins which are located several inches from the center of the shaft and turn in a circle. The crankpins are centered under the cylinders which are machined into the upper block. Aluminum pistons with iron sealing rings are located in the cylinders and are linked to the crankpins via steel connecting rods. The rods connect with the pistons at their upper ends via piston pins and bushings, and at their lower ends fasten to the crankpins around the bearings.

When the crankshaft turns, the pistons move up and down within the cylinders, and the connecting rods convert their reciprocating motion into the rotary motion of the crankshaft. A flywheel at the rear of

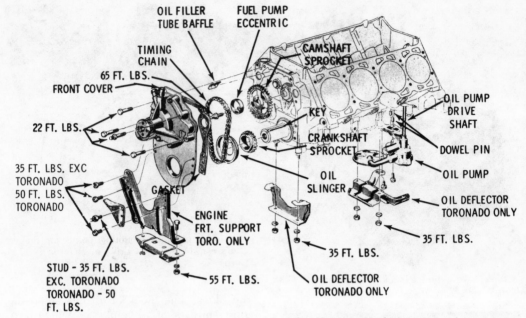

The water and oil pumps are usually mounted directly to the block (© G.M. Corp)

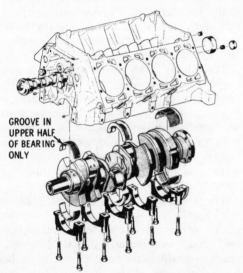

The crankshaft (© G.M. Corp)

A typical piston and rod assembly (© G.M. Corp)

the crankshaft provides a large, stable mass for smoothing out the rotation.

The cylinder heads form tight covers for the tops of the cylinders, and contain machined chambers into which the contents of the cylinders are forced as the pistons reach the upper limit of their travel. Two poppet valves in each cylinder are opened and closed by the action of the camshaft and valve train. The camshaft is driven at one-half crankshaft speed and operates the valves remotely through pushrods and rocker levers via its eccentric lobes or cams. Each combustion chamber contains one intake valve and one exhaust valve.

The cylinder heads also provide mounting threads for spark plugs which screw right through the heads so their lower tips protrude into the combustion chambers.

Lubricating oil, which is stored in a pan

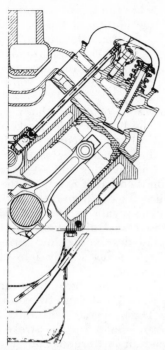

The camshaft operates the valves through push-rods and rocker levers (© G.M. Corp)

at the bottom of the engine and force-fed to almost all the parts of the engine by a gear type pump, lubricates the entire engine and also seals the piston rings.

The engine operates on a four-stroke cycle which is described below.

1. *Intake Stroke:* The intake stroke begins with the piston near the top of its travel, the exhaust valve nearly closed, and the intake valve opening rapidly. As the piston nears the top of its travel and begins its descent, the exhaust valve closes fully, the intake valve reaches a fully open position, and the volume of the combustion chamber begins to increase, creating a vacuum. As the piston descends, an air/fuel mixture is drawn from the carburetor into the cylinder through the intake manifold. (The intake manifold is simply a series of tubes which links each cylinder with the carburetor and the car-

1. Oil pick-up
2. Lifter feed
3. Rocker arm valve tip feed
4. Splash lube to timing chain, fuel pump cam & dist. & oil pump drive
5. Left main gallery feed
6. Cam bearing feed
7. Main bearing feed
8. Rod bearing feed

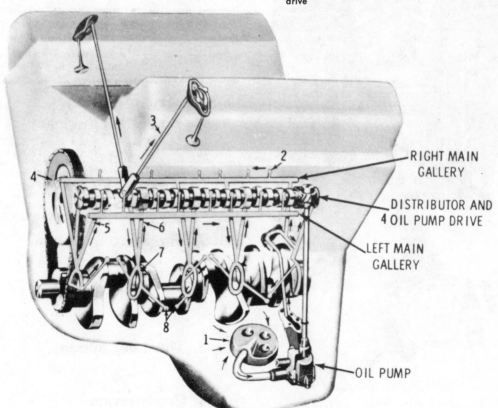

The lubrication system of a large V8 engine (© G.M. Corp)

buretor is a device for using the motion of air moving into the engine to mix just the right amount of fuel into the air stream.) The intake stroke ends with the piston having passed the bottom of its travel. The intake valve reaches a closed position just after the piston has begun its upstroke. The cylinder is now filled with the fuel/air mixture.

2. *Compression Stroke:* As the piston ascends, the fuel/air mixture is forced into the small chamber machined into the cylinder head. This compresses the mixture until it occupies $\frac{1}{8}$th to $\frac{1}{11}$th of the volume that it did at the time the piston began its ascent. This compression raises the temperature of the mixture and increases its pressure, vastly increasing the force generated by the expansion of gases during the power stroke.

3. *Power Stroke:* The fuel/air mixture is ignited by the spark plug just before the piston reaches the top of its stroke so that a very large portion of the fuel will have burned by the time the piston begins descending again. The heat produced by combustion increases the pressure in the cylinder, forcing the piston down with great force.

4. *Exhaust Stroke:* As the piston approaches the bottom of its stroke, the exhaust valve begins opening and the pressure in the cylinder begins to force the gases out around the valve. The ascent of the piston then forces nearly all the rest of the unburned gases from the cylinder. The cycle begins again as the exhaust valve closes, the intake valve opens and the piston begins descending and bringing a fresh charge of fuel and air into the combustion chamber.

Several cars that have been imported into the United States use two-stroke cycle engines. These operate with only a compression stroke and a power stroke. Intake of fuel and air mixture and purging of exhaust gases takes place between the power and compression strokes while the piston is near the bottom of its travel. Ports in the cylinder walls replace poppet valves located in the cylinder heads on four-stroke cycle engines. The crankcase is kept dry of oil, and the entire engine is lubricated by mixing the oil with the fuel so

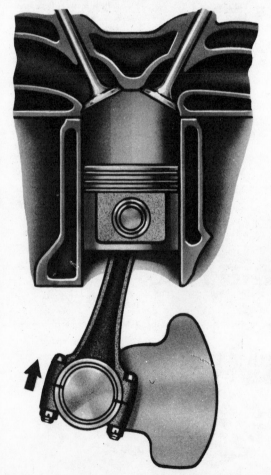

The appearance of the combustion chamber at the beginning of the compression stroke (© G.M. Corp)

Troubleshooting When the Engine Won't Start

Check:

1. The Starting System

↓

2. The Ignition System

↓

3. The Fuel System

↓

4. Compression

that a fine mist of oil covers all moving parts. The ports are designed so the fuel and air are trapped in the engine's crankcase during most of the downstroke of the piston, thus making the crankcase a compression chamber that force-feeds the combustion chambers after the ports are uncovered. The pistons serve as the valves, covering the ports whenever they should be closed.

This should provide a basic understanding of what is going on inside the engine. The ignition, fuel, and engine auxiliary systems will be described later, each in its own troubleshooting section.

2 · The Starting System

How It Works

The battery is the first link in the chain of mechanisms which work together to provide cranking of the automobile engine. In most modern cars, the battery is a lead-acid electrochemical device consisting of six two-volt (2 V) subsections connected in series so the unit is capable of producing approximately 12 V of electrical pres-

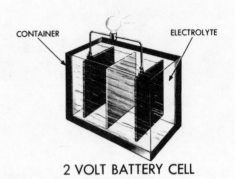

2 VOLT BATTERY CELL

Simplified drawing of a battery cell (Courtesy, Delco-Remy) (© G.M. Corp)

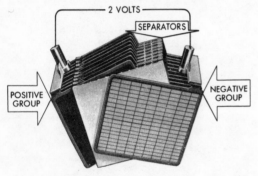

The battery plates which make up one of the six cells (© G.M. Corp)

sure. Each subsection, or cell, consists of a series of positive and negative plates held a short distance apart in a solution of sulfuric acid and water. The two types of plates are of dissimilar metals. This causes

a chemical reaction to be set up, and it is this reaction which produces current flow from the battery when its positive and negative terminals are connected to an electrical appliance such as a lamp or motor. The continued transfer of electrons would eventually convert the sulfuric acid in the electrolyte to water, and make the two plates identical in chemical composition. As electrical energy is removed from the battery, its voltage output tends to drop. Thus, measuring battery voltage and battery electrolyte composition are two ways of checking the ability of the unit to supply power. During the starting of the engine, electrical energy is removed from the battery. However, if the charging circuit is in good condition and the operating

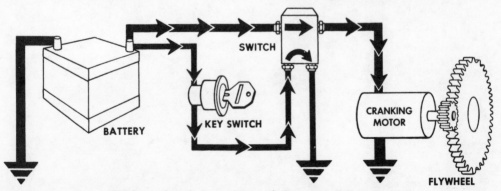

The chain of mechanisms that crank the engine (© G.M. Corp)

8

conditions are normal, the power removed from the battery will be replaced by the generator (or alternator) which will force electrons back through the battery, reversing the normal flow, and restoring the battery to its original chemical state.

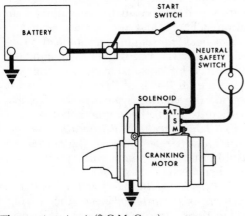

The starting circuit (© G.M. Corp)

The battery and starting motor are linked by very heavy electrical cables designed to minimize resistance to the flow of current. Generally, the major power supply cable that leaves the battery goes directly to the starter, while other electrical system needs are supplied by a smaller cable. During starter operation, power flows from the battery to the starter and is grounded through the car's frame and the battery's negative ground strap.

The starting motor is a specially designed, direct current electric motor capable of producing a very great amount of power for its size. One thing that allows the motor to produce a great deal of power is its tremendous rotating speed. It drives the engine through a tiny pinion gear (attached to the starter's armature), which drives the very large flywheel ring gear at a greatly reduced speed. Another factor allowing it to produce so much power is that only intermittent operation is required of it. Thus, little allowance for air circulation is required, and the windings can be built into a very small space.

The starter solenoid is a magnetic device which employs the small current supplied by the starting switch circuit of the ignition switch. This magnetic action moves a plunger which mechanically engages the starter and electrically closes the heavy switch which connects it to the battery. The starting switch circuit consists of the starting switch contained within the ignition switch, a transmission neutral safety switch or clutch pedal switch, and the wiring necessary to connect these in series with the starter solenoid or relay.

A pinion, which is a small gear, is mounted to a one-way drive clutch. This clutch is splined to the starter armature shaft. When the ignition switch is moved to the "start" position, the solenoid plunger slides the pinion toward the flywheel ring

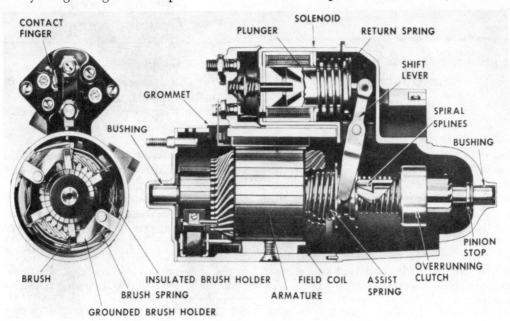

A typical starting motor (© G.M. Corp)

gear via a collar and spring. If the teeth on the pinion and flywheel match properly, the pinion will engage the flywheel immediately. If the gear teeth butt one another, the spring will be compressed and will force the gears to mesh as soon as the starter turns far enough to allow them to do so. As the solenoid plunger reaches the end of its travel, it closes the contacts that connect the battery and starter and then the engine is cranked.

As soon as the engine starts, the flywheel ring gear begins turning fast enough to drive the pinion at an extremely high rate of speed. At this point, the one-way clutch begins allowing the pinion to spin faster than the starter shaft so that the starter will not operate at excessive speed. When the ignition switch is released from the starter position, the solenoid is de-energized, and a spring contained within the solenoid assembly pulls the gear out of mesh and interrupts the current flow to the starter.

Some starters employ a separate relay, mounted away from the starter, to switch the motor and solenoid current on and off. The relay thus replaces the solenoid electrical switch, but does not eliminate the need for a solenoid mounted on the starter used to mechanically engage the starter drive gears. The relay is used to reduce the amount of current the starting switch must carry.

Quick Reference Guide For Starting System Troubleshooting

A. *Inspect the system:* Crank the engine and evaluate the condition of the cranking system by analyzing the response. See the chart of symptoms. If this does not reveal the source of trouble, proceed with the quick checks below. If there is no response but the accessories work, see J.

B. *Make quick checks:* Check the battery terminals and the condition and tension of the fan belt, and evaluate recent operating conditions. If these checks do not reveal the location of the problem, proceed with the more detailed checks below.

C. *Test amperage and voltage:* Check the starter amperage draw in conjunction with battery voltage during cranking. Evaluate the results with the voltage amperage chart.

D. *Check specific gravity of battery cells:* Check the specific gravity of each battery cell and evaluate the battery condition. Charge and replace as necessary.

E. *Check for engine mechanical problems:* Check the viscosity of the engine oil, and check for noises during cranking. Replace the oil if it is of the wrong viscosity. Service the cooling system if the problem exists only when the engine is hot.

F. *Check mechanical condition of the starter and drive:* Remove the starter assembly and check for a stuck pinion gear or other mechanical problems.

G. *Check condition of wiring between battery and starter:* Check the wiring, connections, and switches for high resistance.

H. *Check starter ground circuit:* Check the connections and cable for high resistance.

J. *Check starter switch circuit:* Check the wiring and connections for high resistance. Check switches for continuity and proper linkage operation.

Starting System Troubleshooting

A. Inspect the System:

1. Turn off all accessories. Place manual transmissions in Neutral; automatic transmissions in Park. Depress the clutch pedal all the way on cars with manual transmissions.

2. Turn the ignition switch firmly to the start position. If the engine cranks, hold it there for 15 seconds.

3. If you are familiar with the vehicle, listen for normal starting sounds. If they are unfamiliar, cranking may be checked by looking at the vibration damper on the front of the engine. It should turn steadily at about $1/3$ normal idle speed. Turn on the headlights and check brightness during cranking.

Generally a problem falls into one of the following categories:

a. Starter drive mechanical problems: The starter turns, possibly with a gear clashing noise, but the engine does not turn. The trouble is in the starter pinion or its engagement mechanism, or possibly in the flywheel ring gear. The starter must be removed and the faulty parts repaired or replaced.

b. Engine mechanical problems: The starter turns the engine briefly and then stops very suddenly, or hums but does not turn the engine at all. The engine is hydrostatically locked or has some other severe mechanical defects. Attempt to turn the engine over using an 18 in. flex drive and socket on the crankshaft pulley mounting nut. Inability to turn the engine using this technique confirms the existence of mechanical engine problems. If the engine can be turned but the symptoms above apply, remove the starter and check for starter drive mechanical problems.

c. Malfunction in solenoid switch: The solenoid clicks loudly and the headlights remain bright, but there is no action or noise from the starter motor. The problem is in the solenoid switch and its wiring. Remove the starter and repair the switch.

d. Starter switch circuit: There is no click or other response from starter, but the headlights work normally. Check the starter switch circuit as in section J. If that is not the problem, check G and then H.

e. Bad solenoid: The starter clicks repeatedly, but the lights burn brightly. Check H and I. If no fault is found, replace the solenoid.

f. Bad battery, wiring, or starter: If cranking is sluggish and the lights are dim or the solenoid clicks and the lights are dim, or there is no response at all, follow checks B through J in alphabetical order.

B. Make Quick Checks:

1. Check both battery terminal connections for corrosion. Turn on the headlight switch and watch the headlights while twisting a screwdriver between the cable clamps and terminals, as a further test. If this causes the headlights to brighten, or if the clamps show corrosion, service them as follows: disconnect both clamps, remove corrosion from conducting surfaces, reinstall them securely, and then coat them with petroleum jelly or grease. Avoid the use of force in every way possible. If clamps are bolted together, loosen the nuts

and force the terminals open before removing them. Clamps which are not bolted should be forced on with gentle strokes of a soft mallet. If the starter now cranks properly, return the vehicle to service.

2. Check the tension and condition of the belt(s) which drive the alternator or generator. If there is inadequate tension and belt surfaces are heavily glazed—indicating slippage—replace the belts, tighten them to specifications, recharge the battery, and return the vehicle to service.

3. Evaluate recent operating conditions. If your accessory load has been unusually heavy and the vehicle has been operated at moderate speeds with frequent stops, recharge the battery, and return the vehicle to service. If this is a recurrent problem, the electrical system should be checked for proper generator and regulator performance. In some cases, the regulator can be readjusted to reduce the severity of this problem.

NOTE: *During the tests below, the coil-to-distributor low-tension lead should be disconnected and securely grounded to prevent the vehicle from starting and to protect the ignition system from damage.*

C. Test Amperage and Voltage:

Checking starter amperage draw in conjunction with voltage during cranking will give excellent clues to the nature of the problem.

1. Connect a voltmeter between the positive post of the battery and a good ground.

2. If an induction type starter amperage indicator is available, place the yoke of the meter around a straight section of the cable between the battery and starter. Otherwise, disconnect the battery end of the lead that runs to the starter and securely connect an ammeter of 300 ampere capacity between the battery post and the lead.

A carbon pile rheostat can also be used. Measure voltage during cranking and then connect it in series with the ammeter across the battery terminals. Turn the rheostat until voltage is the same as during cranking. The reading on the ammeter will then show starter draw.

3. Crank the engine for 20 seconds and note the average readings. If you are using

an induction type meter and it reads down-scale, reverse the position of the yoke.

4. Evaluate the readings according to the chart below. On 12 V systems, voltage should be 9.6 or more; on 6 V, 4.8 or more. On 12 V systems, amperage should be 100–200, depending on the size of the engine and its compression ratio. Double the amperages for 6 V systems.

Condition	Voltage	Amperage	Check Section
1	low	normal or low	D
2	near normal	high	E, F °
3	near normal	normal or low	G, H

° NOTE: If sections E and F do not reveal the problem, remove the starter for repair of ground or short circuit.

D. Check Specific Gravity of Battery Cells:

1. Test the specific gravity of each of the battery cells with a battery hydrometer. Do so before attempting to charge the battery. If the battery has been recently charged, or if the electrolyte level is below the level of the plates and requires replenishment, special procedures must be followed to ensure an accurate test. See the section on testing the electrical system for these procedures. Take your measurements carefully, filling and emptying the hydrometer several times to ensure adequate removal of material left in the hydrometer and allowing time for the temperature to come to an accurate reading. Read the gravity scale from the liquid level at the center of the column, not from around the edges where it seeks an abnormally high level. Correct the readings according to the temperature scale on the hydrometer. If a hydrometer and battery thermometer must be used independently, this means subtracting 0.004 for each 10° below 80° F, and adding 0.004 for every 10° above that temperature. Readings not corrected according to temperature are meaningless.

2. Evaluate the readings. A fully

Hydrometer correction chart (Courtesy, Chysler Corp)

charged battery will read between 1.260 and 1.280. Readings must be over 1.220 for the battery to be capable of cranking the engine. If any are below 1.220, or if the readings are far apart, see the section on testing the electrical system for information on evaluating the need for battery replacement or recharging dead batteries. If the battery requires replacement on recharging, be sure to test the charging system before placing the vehicle back in service.

E. Check for Engine Mechanical Problems:

Where amperage is high, a problem may exist in the engine itself or in the starter drive mechanism. If ambient temperature is below freezing, the engine oil should be a multigrade or light straight grade approved for winter use. Normal-weight oil can cause improper cranking in cold weather without any mechanical or electrical malfunction.

1. If improper lubrication is suspected, change the oil (and filter) and refill with the proper grade for the weather conditions. Return the vehicle to service if this permits good cranking.

2. If cranking is accompanied by a mechanical grinding or scraping noise and is very rough and unsteady (not merely sluggish), attempt to rotate the engine using

an 18 in. flex drive and socket on the crankshaft pulley mounting nut. If the engine cannot be rotated or if extreme roughness, or tightness in a sporadic pattern is encountered, mechanical damage is evident. Remove the starter and check for mechanical problems in the starter drive. If none are found, major engine mechanical problems are indicated.

F. Check Mechanical Condition of Starter and Drive:

Where amperage is high and no engine mechanical problems are evident, remove the starter assembly and inspect the pinion and ring gears for sticking or severe wear due to lubrication problems, etc. Also check the starter motor armature shaft bearings. If no mechanical problems are evident, the problem is caused by starter motor or solenoid electrical problems.

G. Check Condition of Wiring Between Battery and Starter:

Normal voltage with low amperage indicates a poor connection somewhere in the starter circuit. The circuit between the battery and starter may be checked as below.

1. Connect the positive lead of a voltmeter (reverse the leads for a negative ground system) to the positive battery terminal. Connect the negative lead to the connector which carries power from the solenoid switch to the starting motor. Crank the engine and take note of the voltmeter reading. The reading should be 0.3 V or less. If the reading is acceptable, proceed to H. Otherwise proceed to step 2.

2. Isolate the faulty component by repeating the test with the voltmeter negative lead connected to each of the following:

a. The starter motor terminal of the solenoid;

b. The battery terminal of the solenoid;

c. Starter terminal of starter relay (if your vehicle has one);

d. Battery terminal of starter relay.

(If the vehicle has a starter relay, it will usually be mounted on one of the fender wells.) The voltage reading should drop slightly as each component is eliminated from the portion of the circuit being tested. If the voltage drops more than 0.1 V when eliminating the solenoid switch or

the relay, the unit is faulty. (Check for burned contacts inside; this is the most common problem.) The resistance of the battery cable should not exceed 0.2 V. Individual connections may be tested for high resistance by placing the probe of the negative lead first on the stud to which the connection is made, and then on the connector on the end of the cable leading to the connection. A measurable difference in the voltage drop indicates a bad connection which must be disassembled and cleaned. Usually bad connections will also be corroded or oil-covered. Be sure, when cleaning, to remove all the oxidized material and to reassemble the connection snugly. A wire brush or sandpaper will help.

H. Check Starter Ground Circuit:

1. Connect the negative lead of the voltmeter to the negative post of the battery (reverse hook-ups for positive ground systems) and the positive lead to a clean, unpainted spot on the starter housing. Crank the engine and note the voltmeter reading. If the reading is higher than 0.2 V, the system may be at fault, and step 2 should be followed. If no defects in the engine, battery, or wiring have been found, the starter should be removed for repair of its electrical circuitry.

2. Repeat the test outlined in step 1 with the positive voltmeter probe connected to:

a. The ground cable to engine or frame connection;

b. The battery negative cable to engine or frame connection;

Individual connections should be tested as in G. The ground cables should have resistances that cause the reading to change less than 0.2 V. Resistance of connections should be negligible.

J. Check Starter Switch Circuit:

1. If the system has a separate starter relay, locate the wire from the starter switch circuit to the relay and disconnect it. If the system uses only a solenoid, locate the wire from the starter switch circuit to the solenoid and disconnect it.

2. If the vehicle has an automatic transmission, make sure it is fully in Neutral or Park. If the vehicle has a manual transmission, the clutch pedal will have to be fully depressed during testing.

3. Connect the positive lead of the voltmeter to the end of the disconnected cable. Have someone turn the ignition switch to the start position and test for voltage. If about 12 V are present, the solenoid or relay is at fault, in most cases. Also check the ground for the relay, or the solenoid-to-starter connection and starter motor ground circuit in systems using a solenoid only.

4. If there is low or no voltage, the problem is in the starter switch circuit. Check for voltage at either side of the neutral safety or clutch pedal safety switch, and for voltage at the ignition switch connection that feeds the starter relay or solenoid. (If the warning lights work, current is getting to the ignition switch.)

When working from the ignition switch toward the starter, the faulty component or connection is between the last point where voltage is detected and the first point which is dead. If the neutral safety switch is a combination type with four prongs, use a jumper cable to find the two prongs which operate the back-up lights, and then test the other prongs only. If the faulty component proves to be the neutral safety switch or clutch switch, remember to check the linkage for proper operation before condemning it. The linkage may be disconnected and moved through the full travel of the switch mechanism while checking for voltage to find out whether or not the fault is in the linkage.

3 · The Ignition System

How It Works

The coil is the heart of the ignition system. It consists of two coils of wire wound about an iron core. These coils are insulated from each other and the whole assembly is enclosed in an oil-filled case. The primary coil is connected to the two primary terminals located on top of the coil and consists of many turns of fine wire. The secondary circuit consists of relatively few turns of a heavier wire and is connected to the high-tension connection on top of the coil. Energizing the coil primary with battery voltage produces current flow through the primary winding; this in turn produces a very large, intense magnetic field. Interrupting the flow of primary current causes the field to collapse. Just as current moving through a wire produces a magnetic field, moving a field across a wire will produce a current. As the magnetic field collapses, its lines of force cross the secondary winding, inducing a current in that winding. The force of the induced current is concentrated because of the relative shortness of the secondary coil of wire.

The distributor is the controlling element of the system, switching the primary current on and off and distributing the current to the proper spark plug each time a spark is produced. It is basically a stationary housing surrounding a rotating shaft. The shaft is driven at one-half engine speed by the engine's camshaft through the distributor drive gears. A cam which is situated near the top of the shaft has one lobe for each cylinder of the engine. The cam operates the ignition contact points, which are mounted on a plate located on bearings within the distributor housing. A rotor is attached to the top of the distributor shaft. When the bakelite distributor cap is in place, on top of the unit's metal housing, a spring-loaded contact connects the portion of the rotor directly above the center of the shaft to the center connection on top of the distributor. The outer end of the rotor passes very close to the contacts connected to the four, six, or eight high-tension connections around the outside of the distributor cap.

Under normal operating conditions, power from the battery is fed through a resistor or resistance wire to the primary circuit of the coil and is then grounded through the ignition points in the distributor. During cranking, the full voltage of the battery is supplied through an auxiliary circuit routed through the solenoid switch. In an eight-cylinder engine, the distributor cam will allow the points to close about 60 crankshaft degrees before the firing of the spark plug. Current will begin flowing through the primary wiring to the positive connection on the coil,

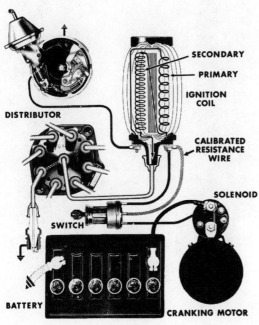

A typical conventional ignition system (© G.M. Corp)

15

**Primary Winding without Current
No Magnetic Field**

**Cutting-in Process
Development of Magnetic Field**

**DC Current in Primary Winding
Constant Magnetic Field**

**Interrupting Process
Collapse of Magnetic Field**

Ignition coil operation (© G.M. Corp)

magnetic field. The condenser consists of several layers of aluminum foil separated by insulation. These layers of foil, upon an increase in voltage, are capable of storing electricity, making the condenser a sort of electrical surge tank. Voltages just after the points open may reach 250 V because of the vast amount of energy stored in the primary windings and their magnetic field. A condenser which is defective or improperly grounded will not absorb the shock from the fast-moving stream of electrons when the points open and these electrons will force their way across the point gap, causing burning and pitting.

The very high voltage induced in the secondary windings will cause a surge of current to flow from the coil tower to the center of the distributor, where it will travel along the connecting strip along the top of the rotor. The surge will arc its way across the short gap between the contact on the outer end of the rotor and the connection in the cap for the high-tension lead of the cylinder to be fired. After passing along the high-tension lead, it will travel down the center electrode of the spark plug, which is surrounded by ce-

through the primary winding of the coil, through the ground wire between the negative connection on the coil and the distributor, and to ground through the contact points. Shortly after the engine is ready to fire, the current flow through the coil primary will have reached a near maximum value, and an intense magnetic field will have formed around the primary windings. The distributor cam will separate the contact points at the proper time for ignition and the primary field will collapse, causing current to flow in the secondary circuit. A capacitor, known as the "condenser," is installed in the circuit in parallel with the contact points in order to absorb some of the force of the electrical surge that occurs during collapse of the

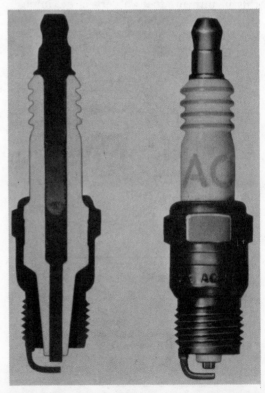

Cross-section of a spark plug. The white portion is the insulator. (© G.M. Corp)

ramic insulation, and arc its way over to the side electrode, which is grounded through threads which hold the plug in the cylinder head. The heat generated by the passage of the spark will ignite the contents of the cylinder.

Most distributors employ both centrifugal and vacuum advance mechanisms to advance the point at which ignition occurs for optimum performance and economy. Spark generally occurs a few degrees before the piston reaches top dead center (TDC) in order that very high pressures will exist in the cylinder as soon as the piston is capable of using the energy—just a few degrees after TDC. Centrifugal advance mechanisms employ hinged flyweights working in opposition to springs to turn the top portion of the distributor shaft, including the cam and rotor, ahead of the lower shaft. This advances the point at which the cam causes the points to open. A more advanced spark is required at higher engine speeds because the speed of combustion does not increase in direct proportion to increases in engine speed, but tends to lag behind at high revolutions. If peak cylinder pressures are to exist at the same point, advance must be used to start combustion earlier.

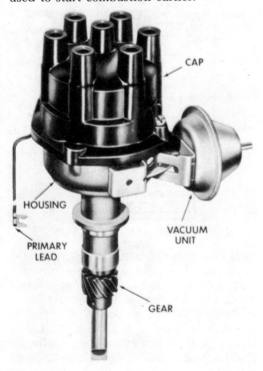

The location of the vacuum advance unit (© G.M. Corp)

Vacuum advance is used to accomplish the same thing when part-throttle operation reduces the speed of combustion because of less turbulence and compression, and poorer scavenging of exhaust gases. Carburetor vacuum below the throttle plate is channeled to a vacuum diaphragm mounted on the distributor. The higher the manifold vacuum, the greater the motion of the diaphragm against spring pressure. A rod between the diaphragm and the plate on which the contact points are mounted rotates the plate on its bearings causing the cam to open the points earlier in relation to the position of the crankshaft.

Quick Reference Guide For Ignition System Troubleshooting

A. *Check for normal cranking.* Correct any deficiencies.

B. *Check for an adequate spark.* If spark is acceptable, proceed to O.

C. *Inspect system for visible deficiencies.* Inspect: primary wiring, secondary wiring, cap, and rotor. Make sure that the distributor shaft turns and the points open and close. If the points are severely burned or do not have the proper gap, remove them, clean with a point file, and reinstall them with the proper gap.

NOTE: *In D through J, the ignition switch should be turned on and the points should be open—unless otherwise indicated.*

D. *Test for voltage at points (with points open).* There should be voltage between the movable breaker arm and ground when the points are open. If there is voltage, proceed to J.

E. *Test for voltage to coil.* If there is no voltage with the ignition switch on, check for voltage during cranking. Voltage only during cranking indicates a bad resistance wire or resistor, in most cases, but the ignition switch should also be suspected.

F. *Test for a ground.* Test for a ground in the coil or another component by disconnecting the lead to the coil positive terminal and checking for amperage between the disconnected lead and the positive terminal with the points open. If there is no amperage, reconnect the wire and proceed to H.

G. *Find the ground.* Reconnect the coil positive wires. Check for amperage between the coil-to-distributor wire (disconnected) and the coil negative terminal. If there is no amperage, replace the coil. If there is amperage, continue to test until the faulty component is isolated.

H. *Test for voltage.* If there is no voltage to the ignition points and no ground exists, test for voltage to find the open circuit. Test at each connection in the circuit. The faulty component will be between a hot connection and a dead connection. If there is no voltage to the coil positive terminal, the problem is between there and the battery.

J. *Check coil polarity.* The polarity of the coil should be the same as the polarity of the battery. If necessary, use a voltmeter and check for negative voltage at the coil tower.

K. *Check coil primary resistance.* Resistance should be 1.0 ohms with external resistor, 4.0 ohms with internal resistor. Replace coil if resistance is not approximately correct.

L. *Check coil secondary resistance.* Resistance should be 4,000–10,000 ohms for a normal-duty coil. Replace if the resistance is outside the acceptable range.

M. *Inspect rotor and cap.* Replace any unserviceable parts and clean as necessary.

N. *Inspect secondary wiring and check its resistance.* Resistance should be about 8,000 ohms per foot.

O. *Clean and gap plugs.* Inspect and replace the plugs if they are defective.

P. *Adjust timing and dwell.* Use a dwell tach, if possible, for the dwell adjustment. Use a stroboscopic timing light, if possible, for the adjustment of ignition timing.

Ignition System
Troubleshooting

A. Check for Normal Cranking.

Turn the ignition switch to the "start" position and check for normal cranking. If cranking is not normal, repair any problems in the starting system before inspecting the ignition system. Low voltage, whether caused by excessive battery drain or poor battery performance, and/or other starter system malfunctions, can affect the performance of the ignition system.

B. Check for an Adequate Spark.

Pull off a spark plug lead and hold it about $3/16$ in. from a good ground. If possible, pull back the rubber boot covering the end of the lead so bare metal is exposed. A good fat spark should appear at regular intervals. Try at least two leads so you can be sure the problem is not just a bad individual cable. If the spark is good, proceed to O. Otherwise, proceed with the checks below.

C. Inspect the System for Visible Deficiencies.

1. Inspect the primary wiring, cap, rotor, and secondary wiring. Look for bad connections, frayed insulation, and grounds in the primary wiring. Look for brittleness, cracks, and carbon tracking in the secondary circuit. Make sure all secondary connections are fully pressed in.

Distributor rotor malfunctions (© G.M. Corp)

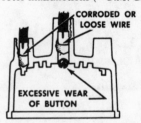

Distributor cap malfunctions (© G.M. Corp)

Correct any deficiencies. Bad wiring must be replaced. A distributor cap or rotor with no cracks and contacts that are still intact may be cleaned in soap and water to remove carbon tracks. Wiring that is wet may be dried with a clean, dry rag or treated with a spray made especially for that purpose.

2. Crank the engine with the distributor cap removed and the high-tension lead to

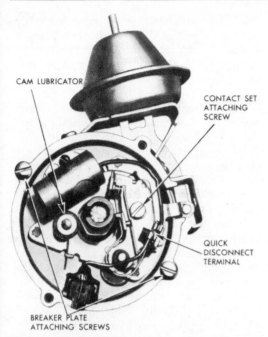

CAM LUBRICATOR

CONTACT SET
ATTACHING
SCREW

QUICK
DISCONNECT
TERMINAL

BREAKER PLATE
ATTACHING SCREWS

The appearance of the ignition points and condenser. The condenser is the cylindrical component. (© G.M. Corp)

the distributor grounded. Check to see that the distributor turns and the points open and close. If the distributor shaft does not turn, the problem is in the drive gear at the lower end of the shaft, and the entire distributor assembly will have to be removed and repaired or replaced.

If the points are severely burned and pitted or they do not have an adequate gap (they should open visibly), remove them, clean them with a point file, and reinstall them. If they are in extremely bad shape, replace them. Repeated excessive burning in less than approximately 12,000 miles points to a faulty condenser or use of the wrong type of condenser. Replace the condenser, if necessary. It may be checked for a short by removing it, and connecting an ohmmeter's leads at the pigtail lead and to the body of the condenser, if malfunction is suspected. The resistance reading will be infinite if the condenser is usable. Points can also burn if the gap (or dwell) is improper, or if an oily gauge has been used to adjust them.

Check the fiber block on the contact points assembly for excessive wear. Excess wear is indicated if it is difficult to adjust the points for a proper gap upon reinstallation, as described below. Make sure the fiber block and cam have a light coating of

clean, high-temperature grease. If they do not, clean and lubricate them carefully. If the fiber block is worn excessively in spite of proper lubrication, or if there is evidence that excessive wear is a problem (timing and dwell go out of adjustment, and the car goes out of tune rapidly), suspect distributor mechanical troubles. Carefully check the cam for roughness or scoring after wiping it clean if this type of problem is suspected. The shaft and bushing wear should also be tested by checking the play in the shaft with a dial indicator. Mechanical problems may also be detected on an electronic distributor tester.

Reinstall the ignition points in their proper position. Using a clean feeler gauge, adjust the position of the stationary contact with the fiber block on the high part of the distributor cam to the specified gap. Unless you are adjusting new points, it will be necessary to avoid contact with built-up material on one of the contact surfaces. A wire gauge may be of help but, in any case, the proper gap must be measured between two parallel surfaces that are neither pitted nor built up with transferred material.

D. Test for Voltage at Points with Points Open.

When the distributor cam is in a position which will hold the points open, the ignition switch is on, and the electrical system is functioning normally in all other respects, there will be approximately 12 V all the way from the battery to the movable contact point. This may be checked by placing the positive probe of a voltmeter on the movable breaker arm and grounding the negative probe. Reverse the polarity for positive ground systems. A test lamp may also be connected between these two spots to make this check. If voltage is good at this point (there should be nearly 12 V if you are using a voltmeter) the primary circuit is in acceptable shape to produce a spark, in most cases, provided the ignition points are not too badly burned. If rotating the distributor until the points close causes the voltage to drop to zero, the points are in functional condition.

If the system passes these two tests, proceed to J. Otherwise, it will be necessary to perform the tests in E. through H. to track down the problem in the primary circuit.

E. Test for Voltage to Coil.

Connect a voltmeter between the positive terminal of the coil and ground following the polarity of the battery. Make sure the ignition switch is turned on. If there is no voltage, jiggle the key, leaving the switch in the "on" position. If voltage appears only when the key is jiggled, the ignition switch is faulty. If jiggling the key has no effect, turn the key to the start position. If this produces voltage at the coil, the problem is most likely the resistor wire that carries current to the coil only when the switch is in the normal running position. If the oil and generator lights do not come on, the problem is most likely in the ignition switch or in the connections on the switch. The switch should be removed and checked for continuity with the internal mechanism set for the "on" position. A wiring diagram will indicate which terminal of the switch receives voltage from the battery and which terminals receive voltage when the switch is on. The connections and the wiring from the battery will have to be checked if the switch has continuity between the proper terminals.

F. Test for a Ground.

Test for a ground in the coil or another component by disconnecting the lead or leads to the coil positive terminal. Test for voltage between each lead and ground. If neither lead is hot, the problem is in the wiring, resistor, or ignition switch, and you should go on to H.

The voltage test in the paragraph above was performed to locate the lead which supplies voltage to the coil while the ignition switch is in the normal running position. Connect an ammeter between that lead and the coil positive terminal. If there is no amperage, proceed to H. If there is amperage, go on to G.

G. Find the Ground.

Reconnect the wires to the coil positive terminal. Disconnect the wire from the coil negative terminal and check for amperage between the terminal and disconnected lead. If there is no amperage, the coil is faulty because of an internal ground and should be replaced.

If there is amperage flowing from the coil to the rest of the system, then there is a ground in the coil-to-distributor wire, or in the points, the condenser or their wiring. Inspect the wires that lead to the points and condenser from the connection inside the distributor. Grounds frequently occur in these wires because they are twisted whenever the vacuum advance diaphragm changes the position of the mounting plate. Grounds will be evidenced by frayed and burned insulation at a spot where the wire contacts the body of the distributor.

If this test reveals no ground, check the condenser for a ground by removing its lead wire and checking for amperage between the connection on the end of the lead and the terminal on the inside of the distributor. If there is any amperage, the condenser is faulty and should be replaced.

If these tests have not located the ground, it is probably in the wire from the coil to the distributor at a spot where it touches metal; in the rubber grommet which carries the primary circuit through the wall of the distributor, in the insulated terminal on the contact points assembly, or in the hinge on the contact points. In most cases, close examination for burning should reveal the location of the problem. If not, testing for amperage as described below may help locate the ground.

Remove the lead from the coil where it connects to the contact point assembly. Test for amperage between the lead's connection and the terminal on the contact assembly. If there is no amperage, the ground must be in the grommet where the primary circuit passes through the distributor, or in the coil-to-distributor wire. Replacing these two parts, which are generally supplied as an assembly, should rectify the problem.

H. Test for Voltage.

The tests above will have revealed whether or not there is voltage to the coil, and will have eliminated the possibility of a ground existing in the circuit. If there is voltage to the positive terminal of the coil, there is an open circuit between there and the ignition points. Otherwise, the problem must be between the ignition coil's positive terminal and the battery.

Proceed in the appropriate direction

from the coil positive terminal, checking for voltage at each connection. The faulty component is between a hot connection and a dead one. For example, if voltage exists at the coil positive terminal, but not at the negative terminal of the coil, the coil must be faulty. Before replacing a component, it might be wise to check it for continuity with an ohmmeter. This will eliminate the chance of mistaking a bad connection for a faulty component. Wiring should have very low resistance (but not zero), and the coil should behave as in K. Keep a sharp eye open for bad connections. Any connection which is dirty, corroded, loose, or burned should be cleaned and tightened.

J. Check Coil Polarity.

While a coil that is connected backward will still produce a spark, weakened ignition system performance will result from improper polarity. If the top of the coil indicates positive and negative terminals, the polarity can be checked visually. The wire coming from the ignition switch should be the same polarity (positive or negative) as the wire going from the battery to the starter, while the coil-to-distributor wire should be the same polarity as the battery ground. If the coil is unmarked, remove the high-tension lead from the coil tower, contact the metal portion of the coil tower with the positive lead of a voltmeter, and ground the voltmeter's negative lead. Crank the engine until a spark is produced. The spark should move the voltmeter's needle downscale. Otherwise, reverse the leads to the coil.

K. Check Coil Primary Resistance.

A weak spark or no spark at all can occur because of an open circuit or ground in either circuit of the coil. The coil can have a very small short or ground which might not show up in general primary system testing but which would have a significant effect on primary circuit resistance.

Disconnect wiring to both primary terminals of the coil. Connect an ohmmeter to the primary circuit—one lead to each primary terminal. The resistance of the coil will depend on whether or not it uses an external ballast resistor. Most coils are externally resisted to permit full battery voltage to be used during cranking. If there are two wires to the positive terminal of the coil, this is a sure sign that the coil is externally resisted. A small component wired in series with the coil in the wire to the positive terminal is another sure sign.

Coils that are externally resisted should have a resistance of approximately 1.0 ohms. Coils that have no external resistor should have about 4.0 ohms resistance. If the resistance is greatly above this figure, or zero (infinite) resistance is indicated, the coil must be replaced.

L. Check Coil Secondary Resistance.

Even if the primary circuit checks out as in K, the coil could be faulty. With the primary leads disconnected, attach an ohmmeter across the secondary circuit of the coil to check for a short or open secondary winding. One probe should go to the metal connector inside the coil tower, while the other *must* go to the positive terminal of the primary circuit. The negative side cannot be used because the secondary is not connected to that side of the primary winding. The resistance should be between approximately 4,000 and 10,000 ohms. These figures are typical of normal-duty coils, but do not apply to heavy-duty equipment. If the resistance is much higher or lower than this, or if it reads zero, replace the coil.

The coil tower should also be checked very carefully for evidence of cracked or burned plastic, or burned metal in the connector inside the tower. Evidence of damage here indicates that the coil should be replaced. If the only burned spot is on the metal conductor, it may be sanded and the coil may be reused, provided the metal is not burned through and a smooth surface can be created.

In cases of coil tower damage, the coil-to-distributor high-tension lead must either be replaced or very carefully checked for burned connectors. If the surface can be smoothed by sanding, the lead may be reused. Use of a bad lead with a new coil can cause recurrence of the burning problem.

M. Inspect Rotor and Cap.

The cap must be gone over with a fine tooth comb to properly check its condition. First, if there is any evidence of carbon, clean the cap carefully in a mild detergent and water solution. After a thorough drying, inspect it very carefully, looking for the following:

1. Looseness of any of the terminals.
2. Excessive burning of any of the terminals.
3. Hairline cracks due to breakage or prolonged arcing.
4. Failure of the spring to push a button type center contact firmly downward.

If the cap is serviceable, sand away any roughness on any of the contacts before reusing it.

Inspect the rotor for any signs of burning, cracking, or breakage. If it uses a spring type of pick-up to contact the carbon button in the center of the cap, make sure there is sufficient tension in the spring for firm contact, bending the pick-up slightly, if necessary. Make sure the contact at the outer end of the rotor is in good condition and will come within about 3/16 in. of the inner surfaces of the terminals in the cap. If the contact surface cannot be smoothed by sanding, replace the rotor.

N. Inspect Secondary Wiring and Check its Resistance.

Inspect all wiring for badly burned connectors, brittleness, or cracks, and replace if any such wear is found. Remove slight burning or roughness with sandpaper.

Connect the probes of an ammeter to either end of each wire to check resistance. It should be approximately 8,000 ohms per foot. Replace high-resistance wire. This, of course, includes wire that shows zero resistance, indicating a completely open circuit.

O. Clean and Gap the Spark Plugs.

Badly burned spark plugs can cause misfiring, poor gas mileage, and difficult starting. Clean any carbon and lead deposits off both electrodes so a good inspection can be made. A relatively soft wire brush is the best tool for this job and is available as a part of many combination feeler gauge and spark plug tools.

The side electrode should be square and uniform in shape along its entire length and should extend well over the center of the center electrode. Burning will shorten this electrode and round it off near the free end. The center electrode should be uniform in diameter (not burned thinner near the top) and should form a relatively

flat surface under the side electrode. A very round top surface, or only slight extension above the insulator, indicates extreme burning. The insulator should be smooth and round, entirely free of cracks, and tightly molded in place. If shaking the plug up and down causes the insulator to move up and down, it is severely damaged. Replace plugs which show any evidence of burning or damaged insulators.

The outer insulator should also be inspected for cracks after a thorough cleaning. Any evidence of cracking or arcing here means the plug is defective.

If the plugs are severely burned, the problem is usually one of the four below:

1. Improper torquing in the head, meaning poor cooling.
2. Use of a plug of too high a heat range.
3. Advance ignition timing, or lean carburetion.
4. Extremely prolonged use.

See the section on correcting poor engine operation for additional information.

If the plugs are in good condition, they may be reused if they are thoroughly cleaned and properly gapped to the manufacturer's specifications. A wire feeler gauge must be used to set the gap. The gap is correct when a slight pull is required to free the gauge from between the two electrodes. Bend the side electrode

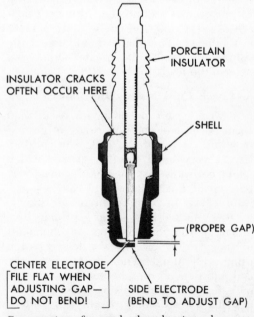

Cross-section of a spark plug showing where gap is to be measured (© G.M. Corp)

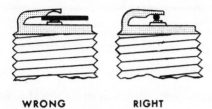

WRONG   **RIGHT**

Proper gapping of spark plugs (© G.M. Corp)

only when closing or opening the gap, using a spark plug tool. The gap should be set according to the manufacturer's specifications, which can be found on the sticker under the hood on post-1967 cars. Full-size American engines usually use a 0.035 in. gap. Smaller gaps are used with most smaller engines. Reinstall the plugs, using new gaskets, and torque to approximately 14 ft lbs for 10 mm plugs, or 30 ft lbs for 14 mm plugs. Use 3 ft lbs less, in either case, for engines with aluminum heads.

P. Adjust Timing and Dwell.

The dwell angle is the amount of time, measured in degrees of distributor shaft rotation, that the contact points remain closed. Dwell angle is an indirect measurement of point gap. Increasing the point gap will decrease the dwell angle, as the cam will then separate the points earlier and allow them to close later. Decreasing the point gap will increase the dwell angle as the points will then be in contact with the distributor cam for a shorter period of time.

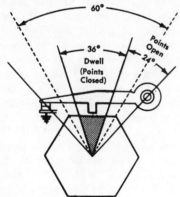

Dwell angle (© G.M. Corp)

Ignition timing refers to the point in the rotation of the engine when ignition occurs. It is measured in degrees of crankshaft rotation in relation to TDC in number one cylinder when the cylinder is on the compression stroke. Timing is gener-

ally set at an engine speed which requires no centrifugal or vacuum advance, although in some cases vacuum retarding action is in effect.

The dwell angle *must* be set before the timing is adjusted and must *never* be disturbed unless timing is reset immediately thereafter. While ignition timing has no effect on dwell angle, a dwell change will affect timing because the distributor cam will separate the points at a different point in the rotation of the distributor shaft after the dwell adjustment.

Adjust timing and dwell as follows:

1. Connect a dwell-tach to the ignition system with the engine off. The negative or black clip goes to a good ground, while the positive or red clip should be attached to the negative (distributor) terminal of the coil primary circuit.

2. Make sure the wires are away from the fan and other engine auxiliaries. Start the engine and place it in or out of gear, as the manufacturer recommends on the engine compartment sticker or in a manual. If setting the timing requires disconnecting the vacuum lines, etc., perform these operations before setting the dwell. Switch the dwell tach to the tachometer function and to the proper setting for the number of cylinders in the engine. Making sure you are reading the right scale, check to see if the idle speed is as specified for setting the timing. Dwell should be set at this speed because some distributors on late-model cars change their dwell settings as rpm changes. Adjust the idle speed if it is not as specified.

3. Switch the dwell-tach over to the dwell function and read the dwell angle. If

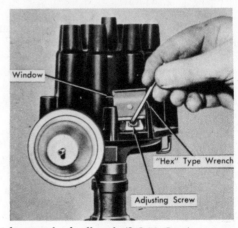

Adjusting the dwell angle (© G.M. Corp)

the dwell is outside the range specified by the manufacturer, adjust it.

4. Readjust the dwell, increasing the point gap if the dwell angle is too large, and decreasing it if the angle is too small. On some distributors, this may be done with an allen wrench through a window in the side of the distributor while the engine is running.

5. Turn off the engine and locate number one (no. 1) cylinder. Most engine blocks (or intake manifolds) are marked. Number one cylinder is usually the front one on inline engines, or the right front one on V8 engines. The timing light is usually connected by inserting a high-tension connection between the no. 1 plug and its wire and then connecting two 12 V leads to the battery—red to positive; black to negative. Making sure that no wires are near the fan, start the engine and, if necessary, put the transmission in gear.

The timing mark and scale (© G.M. Corp)

6. Aim the timing light at the pulley on the front of the engine. The timing mark, which is usually a groove in the outer flange of the pulley, should be visible each time the timing light flashes. It may be necessary to stop the engine and mark the groove with chalk if visibility is poor.

7. Line up the timing mark with the scale, pointer, or mark on the engine. If necessary, loosen the distributor locking bolt and turn it until the pulley mark aligns with the proper mark on the engine. (Check the manufacturer's specifications.) Tighten the locking bolt and recheck the timing before shutting off the engine.

Electronic Ignition Systems

How They Work

Electronic ignition systems use the same type of ignition coil to generate a hot spark, and employ the same type of rotor, distributor cap, wiring, and spark plugs to provide that spark to the cylinders. The main difference is that they employ a transistor to start and stop the flow of primary current.

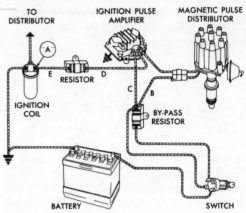

Diagram of a General Motors electronic ignition system (© G.M. Corp)

A transistor is a solid-state relay. This means that it can start and stop the flow of electric current without the use of moving parts. It is turned on and off by a current much smaller than that required to energize a coil. Thus, the problems associated with ignition point burning and wear can be vastly reduced if the ignition points are used to supply the signal to the transistor. Because the signal to the transistor is so small, the points can even be replaced by a simple type of signal generator which uses a permanent magnet and the motion of the distributor shaft to generate the signal in a pick-up coil without any mechanical contact or direct passage of current.

The switching transistor is part of an amplifier unit, which, in several stages, amplifies the original signal supplied by the pick-up coil, in some units. In others, a capacitor is first charged, and then is discharged across the primary circuit of the coil when ignition is required.

Electronic Ignition Troubleshooting

The troubleshooting procedure that must be followed is different for each type of electronic ignition system. Since this book is intended to cover troubleshooting as it applies generally to a number of different types of automobiles, specific procedures for troubleshooting each type of system are beyond its scope.

Many problems can, however, be detected by following the troubleshooting chart in the previous section as modified below:

C. If the system uses a pick-up coil, make sure the coil and reluctor (the rotating part on the shaft) are not hitting each other. Adjust a Chrysler coil until it is 0.010 in. from the reluctor.

D.–H. If the system uses a pick-up coil, check for voltage at various connections. Check the resistors for continuity with an ohmmeter.

K.–L. Coil resistances may be slightly outside the specified ranges for primary and secondary circuits. Open circuits will still be indicated, however, by zero resistance.

P. Dwell is not adjustable on systems that do not use conventional contact points.

4 · The Fuel System

How It Works

The fuel burned in a gasoline engine is a mixture of hydrocarbon liquids—all with different boiling points. The purpose of the fuel system is to mix the proper amount of fuel with the air that the engine demands, effectively evaporate most of the fuel, and conduct the air/fuel mixture to the engine cylinders. The fuel system also regulates the flow of mixture to the engine for control of power output.

The fuel is stored in a tank which generally serves to allow for settling of water and other foreign material by picking up the fuel several inches off the bottom of the tank. A strainer is frequently used in the pick-up inside the tank.

Most engines employ a mechanical fuel pump which is driven by an eccentric on the camshaft. The pump is a flexible diaphragm mounted inside a housing. The eccentric on the camshaft forces the diaphragm down for intake of fuel and a spring forces the diaphragm back up. When fuel is not required by the carburetor, the spring remains compressed and the diaphragm remains motionless during what would normally be a discharge

stroke for the pump. A line connects the fuel pick-up in the tank with the pump so the suction created by the pump can pull fuel from the tank to the pump inlet. A similar line connects the pump outlet to the carburetor. Some vehicles use electrically driven pumps that operate much as the engine-driven pump, but use solenoids to move the pump diaphragm up and down. A few vehicles employ in-tank centrifugal, electrical pumps.

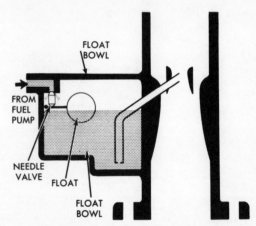

The carburetor float system (© G.M. Corp)

The carburetor stores the fuel in a vented tank known as the "float bowl." A float-operated valve maintains the level of fuel in the bowl within a narrow range. As the fuel level rises, the float will rise and close off the valve, thus causing the movement of the fuel pump diaphragm to be reduced because of reduced discharge of fuel.

The carburetor handles all the air which the engine receives and regulates its flow through the action of a throttle. The air passes through a slight restriction in the carburetor, known as a "venturi." The venturi causes some of the atmospheric pressure that is pushing the air to be lost as the air speeds up in passing through the restriction. The pressure in the venturi

A typical carburetor (© G.M. Corp)

drops as the air flow increases. In order to improve the accuracy of the metering at low speeds, a booster venturi is frequently used. It is a much smaller venturi, mounted above the regular one, in the center of the carburetor bore.

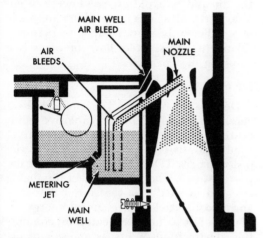

The carburetor main circuit (© G.M. Corp)

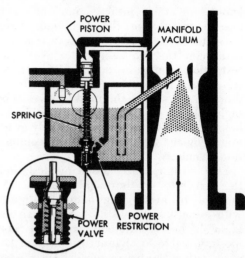

The carburetor power system (© G.M. Corp)

A main metering system, consisting of a nozzle and a discharge tube which carries the fuel to a spot inside the venturi in the throttle bore, conducts the fuel to the airstream during most driving conditions. Since vacuum in the venturi is proportional to the amount of air passing through it, the air/fuel ratio is fairly accurately governed by the amount of vacuum available to lift fuel from the bowl to the discharge. If the carburetor uses a booster venturi, fuel is discharged at the center of the booster to provide the best possible metering at low speeds. The arm which carries fuel to the booster venturi and supports it is usually integral with several other carburetor parts, such as idle or accelerator pump passages. The assembly is known as the "venturi cluster" and can be separated from the main body of the carburetor during disassembly. In some carburetors, a metering rod, which is positioned by the throttle linkage, throttles the flow of fuel through the main discharge nozzle for increased metering accuracy.

The flow of fuel through the main nozzle is supplemented at very high throttle openings by a power enrichment system that provides sufficient fuel to ensure fullest use of the air inducted by the engine at full power conditions. This system consists of an auxiliary fuel passage and metering valve on carburetors which do not employ

metering rods, and an auxiliary metering rod positioning mechanism on those which do. In either case, a piston is kept in an inactive position by high manifold vacuum. When manifold vacuum becomes very low, as at full throttle, the piston either opens the valve in the auxiliary fuel passage, or, in the case of units using metering rods, moves the rod slightly further out of the main metering nozzle, or "jet." A spring generally forces the system to operate when manifold vacuum drops off.

The carburetor also employs an idle passage which conducts fuel from the float bowl to a spot below the throttle. When the throttle is nearly shut, the vacuum created in the venturi is negligible, but manifold vacuum under the throttle is very high, and pulls the fuel required at idle through this small auxiliary system. Flow of fuel through this system is adjustable by a mixture screw accessible from outside the carburetor.

The carburetor also employs a pump that is operated by the throttle linkage to discharge a spray of fuel into the airstream during sudden increases in throttle opening. This pump provides instant response to sudden changes in conditions.

Many carburetors use two or four venturis to provide better distribution of fuel to the engine or to permit progressive use of two sets of venturis for more accurate metering of fuel over a wider range of air flow conditions.

The fuel is conducted by a series of tubes from the carburetor to the intake ports of the engine block. These tubes are known as the "intake manifold" and branch away from the carburetor base. Small tubes are used all the way from the carburetor to each cylinder to avoid the restriction to mixture flow that would result if large ducts were suddenly narrowed down to the size of the intake valves. The high velocity in the intake manifold also helps the fuel to be more completely evaporated by the time it reaches the combustion chambers.

Evaporation is also aided by designing the carburetor to thoroughly atomize the fuel and by heating the manifold slightly with exhaust manifold heat. Some exhaust manifold heating systems employ a thermostatic valve to channel the flow of hot gases either toward or away from the intake manifold walls depending on temperature conditions.

During cold-engine operating conditions, evaporation of fuel is very poor. The carburetor uses a choke to permit smooth cold-engine operation. The choke is constructed much like the throttle, but is located above the venturi so that closing it will produce a vacuum that will increase the amount of fuel flowing from the carburetor jets into the air stream. This very rich mixture will contain sufficient fuel to provide a combustible mixture, even though the cold temperatures will retard the evaporation process.

The choke is operated by a thermostatic spring, the tension of which is relaxed by heat from the exhaust manifold as the engine warms up. Intake manifold vacuum also affects the position of the choke, which is mounted off center in the carburetor bore. Increased flow of air will thus tend to open the choke and maintain a fairly even vacuum at the fuel metering jets. A vacuum-operated diaphragm may also be used to prevent cold operation

from being excessively rich. The diaphragm is linked to the choke through a lever arm and opens the choke slightly as soon as there is a vacuum in the manifold.

An air cleaner is mounted on top of the carburetor to remove dust and dirt from the air and to avoid excessive wear of engine parts. Most recent air filters are made of a sufficiently porous paper to permit a relatively unrestricted flow of air while catching dust particles.

DETONATION

Detonation, or "knock" or "ping," is a severely damaging form of explosive combustion. During normal engine operation, combustion is only partly complete as the piston passes TDC at the beginning of the power stroke. The full energy of the fuel is released gradually as the piston descends and is converted to mechanical energy almost as fast as heat is created by combustion. Detonation occurs as a result of extreme temperatures and pressures in the cylinders. Cylinder temperatures become so high that the pressure increase caused by combustion near the spark plug raises a great portion of the total charge to a temperature above its ignition point, causing simultaneous combustion at many points in the chamber rather than the normal gradual spreading of the flame. The result is a violent shock to the piston and cylinder walls and searing heat.

Gasoline octane rating refers to the ability of the fuel to resist rapid combustion of the type that damages the engine. Detonation may be caused by use of the wrong spark plug, an incorrect fuel mixture, improper ignition timing, or overheating. However, by far the most common cause, assuming the engine is reasonably well maintained, is use of a fuel of too low an octane rating. Use a reputable brand of

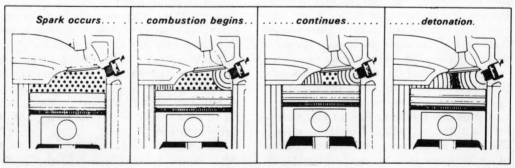

Detonation

gasoline of regular or premium grade, depending on the manufacturer's recommendations for the particular engine. In some cases, this will still result in slight detonation because of variations in individual engines. A fuel with sufficient antiknock quality should be used to avoid audible detonation.

VAPOR LOCK AND PERCOLATION

Vapor lock is the evaporation of fuel into vapor due to heat conducted to the fuel pump. This vapor paralyzes the pump. The pump has only limited ability to handle gaseous material. The vapor simply expands and contracts as the diaphragm operates, rather than flowing in and out. Some air-conditioned cars have a return line designed to allow fuel vapor to be shunted back to the fuel tank.

Percolation is a related phenomenon, but occurs in the carburetor. Fuel vapor formed by heat increases the pressure in the float bowl, causing it to overflow into the throttle bores. Flooding problems result when the engine is hot.

Quick Reference Guide For Fuel System Troubleshooting

A. *Inspect the system.* Make sure there is fuel in the tank. Remove the air cleaner and check it for clogging. Clean or replace it as necessary. Check the choke for freedom of operation and proper response to temperature conditions. See subsection F. if the choke appears to be malfunctioning. Check the throttle bores for the presence of excess fuel. Check for fuel in the carburetor by operating the throttle linkage and looking for accelerator pump discharge. If there is no discharge, check further by cranking the engine with one of the spark plug leads disconnected, and then removing a spark plug to check for the presence of fuel. Tap the carburetor bowl sharply several times, then crank the engine with the high-tension lead connected to check for relief of the flooding or no-fuel condition. If this permits the engine to start, go directly to subsection G. Check all accessible carburetor mounting nuts and screws for tightness.

B. *Check the fuel supply system.* Disconnect the fuel line at the carburetor. Crank the engine and collect fuel in a clean glass container. If the fuel volume appears to be adequate and the fuel is clean, see subsection C. and then skip D. and E. if pump pressure is adequate. If the fuel contains water, drain the tank and refill it with clean fuel. If fuel volume is minimal and there are bubbles, see D.

C. *Check pump output pressure.* Pressure should be approximately 3–7 lbs. If pressure and volume are all right, go to subsection F.

D. *Check pump suction.* Check for loose connections at the pump inlet and fuel tank. Check the pump's ability to pull vacuum. It should pull about 15 in. If vacuum is inadequate, the pump must be replaced. If vacuum is adequate but pressure and volume problems are evident, check the strainers and lines as in E. Replace the pump only if these checks do not improve performance.

E. *Check strainers and lines.* Check the condition of the fuel tank strainer and clean it if necessary. Blow out the tank-to-pump and pump-to-carburetor lines. Check all lines for cracks or bad fittings. Check and clean the carburetor strainer if necessary. If the fuel pump has a strainer, check it and, if necessary, clean it.

F. *Check the choke and throttle linkages.* Make sure the throttle linkage works freely and permits the throttle to open fully. Check the choke for freedom of operation and proper response. Correct any binding and check all adjustments.

G. *Check for carburetor internal problems.* If sticking of the float was noted in A., it would be wise to attempt treating the carburetor with a solvent first to avoid unnecessary disassembly. Remove the carburetor and disassemble it. Make the following checks:

1. Float level and drop, and the condition of all related parts.

2. Mounting and cleanliness of venturi cluster.

3. Metering valve or power system valve adjustment, and the condition of parts.

4. Appearance of the fuel in the bowl. Check for leakage in the bowl.

5. Accelerator pump condition and adjustments.

6. Condition of throttle shafts and bores and cleanliness of jets.

H. Check for miscellaneous fuel system problems, which cause bad idle, vapor lock, stalling, or running on. Check manifold bolts, idle speed, idle mixture, and solenoid or dashpot operation. Check for leaks in the intake system, and check the function of the PCV system. Check the operation of the manifold heat control valve. Check for proper routing of the fuel lines.

Fuel System Troubleshooting

A. Inspect the System.

Make sure there is fuel in the tank. Turn on the ignition switch and look at the gauge. If the gauge responds normally and reads anywhere but at the extremes, there is probably fuel in the tank. Unless you're sure that there is fuel in the tank, gently push a clean, slender object down the tank filler to check. If fuel level cannot be clearly determined in this way, the best procedure is to put a gallon or two of fuel in to ensure the pick-up is covered.

Remove the air cleaner to check its condition. It should be possible to see a bright light through a paper element. If the element is dirty, blow the dirt off from the inside with air pressure. If this will not do an adequate cleaning job, the filter element should be replaced.

An oil bath unit will rarely clog enough to severely restrict air flow but it would be wise to clean a very dirty unit by dipping it in a solvent and moving it back and forth until the dirt has been effectively removed. Drain the oil from the base, remove the residue with solvent, and refill the base to the mark with clean engine oil. Do not reinstall the air cleaner until the fuel system problem has been found.

Open the throttle slightly to allow the automatic choke to set itself, and then check its position. If the engine is dead cold, and the outside temperature is as low as 70° F, the choke will generally close fully. The choke should be wide open at operating temperature. At temperatures in between these extremes, the choke should seek a middle position. After observing the position of the choke, move the flap very gently back and forth holding the throttle part-way open. If the choke does not come

to an appropriate position, or if it does not move freely, see F.

Check for flooding next. Inspect the throttle bores for the presence of liquid fuel. If there is an obvious smell of raw fuel and the bores are lined with liquid, the engine is flooded. Flooding may be caused by improper starting technique—primarily, pumping of the throttle. If this is not suspected, tap the carburetor bowl firmly with a light but solid object, and then crank the engine for 20–30 seconds with the throttle held firmly to the floor. If this procedure allows the car to start, the problem is a stuck float. If the carburetor was flooded, see subsection C. on checking fuel pump pressure, and then go to subsection G.

To test for the presence of fuel in the carburetor, move the throttle from idle position to full throttle while watching for accelerator pump discharge. If there is no discharge, check further before assuming there is no fuel in the carburetor. Disconnect one of the spark plug leads. Crank the engine for 15–20 seconds with the throttle slightly open. Immediately pull the spark plug where the lead was disconnected. Check the electrodes for the presence of fuel. If the electrodes are dry, either the carburetor is malfunctioning or there is no fuel getting to it. Tap the carburetor bowl several times with a light but solid object, and then replace the spark plug and repeat the test. If this puts noticeable amounts of fuel on the plug's electrodes or enables the engine to start, the problem is a stuck float and subsection G. should be consulted without going through the others. Go to G. also, if the accelerator pump discharges fuel.

B. Check the Fuel Supply System.

Disconnect the fuel line at the carburetor. Ground the distributor high-tension lead. Crank the engine for about 15 seconds with a clean glass container held under the open end of the fuel line. Fuel should be discharged regularly and forcefully, and it should not contain bubbles. If the discharge is minimal, see D. and E. to find out whether the problem is in the pump or lines. If there are bubbles, see E.

The fuel collected in the glass should be carefully inspected for the presence of water and dirt. If very small water bubbles are present, the fuel in the tank may be treated with any of several products designed to make the water mix with the gas and thus be eliminated from the system. If a layer of water is formed on the bottom of the glass, the fuel system must be thoroughly cleaned as follows:

1. Drain the gas tank. Drains are provided on many tanks for removal of the water and dirt which tend to accumulate there. If no drain is provided, the fuel line will have to be disconnected, and the tank will have to be dismounted so the water and dirt can be drained out the filler pipe. The tank should be flushed with clean fuel before replacing the fittings and restoring it to service.

2. Check the condition of the fuel tank strainer, generally located in the pick-up and fuel gauge assembly, and replace it if it is damaged.

3. Blow out the tank-to-pump line and the pump-to-carburetor line with compressed air.

C. Check Pump Output Pressure.

The pressure may be checked by removing the pump discharge line and connecting a pressure gauge to the pump outlet. There are many gauges on the market for testing fuel pump pressure, manifold vacuum, etc. These employ a connector of standard size which will fit into most fuel pump discharge openings.

A check of pump output pressure will determine the ability of the pump to force fuel to the carburetor, and also check its ability to draw fuel from the tank, and the ability of the tank-to-pump lines to supply it, provided a good discharge volume was noted in B. Most fuel pumps are rated at engine idle speed. If the engine will run, it is best to connect all fuel and ignition lines, start the engine, and allow it to run to fill the carburetor float bowl. Disconnect the fuel line at the pump, hook up the test gauge, and restart the engine, running it at slow idle on the fuel in the float bowl. If the engine will not run, pump operation at cranking speeds will give an indication of whether or not the pump will function well enough to permit the engine to start.

Fuel pump pressures generally range from three to seven pounds. Three pounds will at least supply the carburetor with adequate fuel for starting the engine. At idle speed, however, the pump pressure should be within the range specified by the manufacturer; either low or high pressures can cause operating problems.

If the fuel pump pressure is all right, be sure to check the pump-to-carburetor fuel line and carburetor strainer for clogging. Then go to F.

D. Check Pump Suction.

A check of fuel pump suction will reveal whether or not the pump is faulty. Low output pressure can also result from a restriction or leak in the suction lines.

Disconnect *both* the pump discharge and inlet lines. The discharge is disconnected so there is no chance that a restriction in the line or carburetor strainer, or a normally functioning carburetor float, could restrict pump discharge and prevent the pump from developing its full suction power.

Connect a vacuum gauge to the pump, using an appropriate piece of rubber hose. Crank the engine until the gauge reaches a stable reading. It should be 15 in. or over. If not, the pump is faulty, and should be replaced.

A pump that will pull 15 in. of vacuum *can* be faulty. If checking and cleaning the strainers and lines as in E. does not result in good fuel pump performance, replace the pump.

E. Check Strainers and Lines.

If the fuel pump output pressure is inadequate, but the pump is capable of pulling a good vacuum, the fuel lines are most likely clogged or kinked, or the fuel system fittings are loose or cracked. A careful visual inspection of all accessible parts of the system should be made before the difficult-to-reach parts are checked out. The fitting at the fuel pump suction side should be very carefully inspected for cracks or deterioration. If a flexible hose is used here, the hose should be crack-free and firm in order to resist collapsing, and it must be equipped with good clamps. Replace any doubtful parts. The entire length of the fuel lines along the frame to the fuel tank should be checked for the presence of kinks or dents that might have come from improper installation or road damage. The fuel line should then be removed from the tank and blown out with compressed air or replaced, as necessary. The fuel tank strainer should be inspected to ensure that it is clean and properly installed.

The fuel pump-to-carburetor line should also be checked for kinks, cracks, or bad fittings, and blown out with compressed air. The fuel strainer in the carburetor should be checked for cleanliness and cleaned or replaced as necessary. If the vehicle employs an inline fuel filter or strainer, be sure to check its condition and connections.

F. Check the Choke and Throttle Linkages.

An inoperative throttle linkage could prevent starting by keeping the choke from closing during cranking or failing to supply adequate fuel/air mixture. Also, inadequate performance can frequently be traced to a linkage which does not open the throttle all the way. Have someone depress the accelerator pedal to the floor while you watch the throttle blade. It should reach a perfectly vertical position as the accelerator pedal reaches the floor. Adjustable linkages usually employ some sort of clamp or turnbuckle arrangement which is easily adjusted. Nonadjustable types that do not provide proper throttle operation usually perform improperly because of a bent bracket or a stretched cable.

Some four-barrel carburetors employ special air valves at the tops of their bores for controlling the metering of fuel. Check to see that the shafts which bear these valve flaps turn freely in their bores. Disassemble them and clean the shaft and the shaft bores if there is binding.

If a four-barrel carburetor uses vacuum diaphragm actuation of the secondary bores, the throttles must be observed with the engine running and air cleaner removed. At full-throttle position and high rpm, the secondary throttles should open fully. If they do not operate properly, check for binding or a leaky vacuum diaphragm.

An improperly functioning automatic choke is one of the most frequent causes of difficult starting. Because it operates through a delicate balance of carburetor air and thermostatic spring pressures, its tolerance to the accumulation of dirt is very low. Its delicate mechanism is also easily damaged.

An excellent indication of choke condition is its position when the engine is cold. Remove the air cleaner, open the throttle wide to release the choke mechanism from the fast idle cam, and observe what the choke does. It should close all the way if the engine is cold and the outside temperature is 70° or below. Under higher temperature conditions, the choke will generally be part-way closed until the engine thermostat opens (hot water is present in both radiator hoses). If the choke does not respond properly, it should be cleaned very carefully with solvent, and inspected for bent or broken linkage parts. The most effective procedure is to remove the screws that hold the choke flap to the choke (being *very* careful not to drop them down the carburetor throat), unfasten and remove the various parts of the linkage, usually simple metal clips, and pull the shaft and flap out of the carburetor throat. The shaft should be checked for bending, a very common cause of choke binding, and the shaft and the shaft bores in the carburetor very thoroughly cleaned of dirt and carbon deposits. If the choke uses a choke piston, located within the body of the carburetor, particular attention should be paid to determining that the piston and bore are clean, as this is another place binding can occur as a result of accumulated dirt.

During reassembly, all parts of the mechanism should be thoroughly checked to make sure no binding will occur due to bent parts. For example, if a U-shaped link is used in the mechanism, the center portion of the link should be straight, and the two ends should be parallel. There is a secondary air valve lockout, on four-barrel carburetors, which rides along a pin located on the choke flap, parallel to the shaft. This can be bent during air cleaner installation and can cause binding of the choke. In either of these cases, the choke will malfunction even though all parts may be perfectly clean. The watchword is thoroughness. No part of the choke linkage should be above suspicion, and all parts should be carefully removed and inspected.

The same kind of care pays off in the cleaning process. Disassemble the linkage wherever one part turns on another. Treat the unit with solvent and wipe with a clean rag or paper towel to remove any grime loosened by the solvent.

After the mechanism is reassembled, several checks of choke operation should

GUM AND VARNISH DEPOSITS

Spots where gum and varnish form on carburetors using choke pistons (Courtesy, Chrysler Corp)

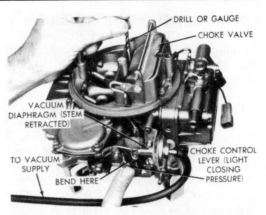

DRILL OR GAUGE
CHOKE VALVE
VACUUM DIAPHRAGM (STEM RETRACTED)
TO VACUUM SUPPLY
BEND HERE
CHOKE CONTROL LEVER (LIGHT CLOSING PRESSURE)

A typical factory manual illustration giving instructions on choke vacuum break adjustment (Courtesy, Chrysler Corp)

be made. These are best made with a factory manual or *Chilton's Auto Repair Manual.* These manuals contain specific instructions on the proper method of adjusting the various linkages and the proper specifications. Some cursory checks and adjustments can be made, however.

1. Choke coil operation. It would be wise to remove and inspect the choke coil. If the coil is housed in a circular chamber which is rotated to make the basic choke adjustment, mark the position of the chamber so it can be replaced in its original position. Remove the choke thermostatic coil housing and inspect the coil to make sure it is intact and clean. If there is evidence of corrosion, replace the choke heat tube or heat well so exhaust gases cannot continue to enter the coil housing. If the engine is hot, a rough check of choke coil adjustments can be made by placing the coil and housing in a cool spot until they have reached room temperature, and then quickly putting them in place on the carburetor, opening the throttle, and watching the choke. If the choke does not close fully, a slight twisting of an adjustable housing or a slight bend of the choke actuating rod, if the housing is not adjustable, will usually correct the problem. Move the choke flap to the wide open position to make sure the adjustment will not keep the choke from opening fully.

2. Choke vacuum break operation. The choke vacuum break is operated by the intake manifold vacuum created when the engine starts, and is placed on the carburetor to eliminate overly rich operation just after the engine has been started from

cold. If the vehicle starts properly, but tends to run richly and smoke for the first few minutes of driving, the choke vacuum break may be at fault. The function of the vacuum diaphragm may be checked by starting the engine and allowing it to idle. Under these conditions, the vacuum diaphragm should recede into the housing and seat firmly. Check to see that this motion will pull the choke part-way open by forcing it toward the closed position until all the play in the linkage is removed and the diaphragm is keeping the choke from moving farther. To check this adjustment precisely, refer to a manual for instructions. These instructions will usually specify that the choke flap must be a certain distance from the front wall of the throttle bore with all the play in the linkage removed and the vacuum diaphragm firmly seated. The wire link between the vacuum diaphragm and the choke linkage is usually bent at the bottom of a U-shaped section to adjust the linkage. The vacuum diaphragm may be seated by running the engine, employing a vacuum pump on the end of the vacuum diaphragm hose, or by gently holding the diaphragm in the withdrawn position by hand. Using vacuum is preferable to handling the delicate mechanism, and guarantees that the diaphragm will be fully seated, if at least 15 in. of vacuum is employed.

If the vacuum diaphragm does not function, check for a cracked or loose hose, a plugged carburetor port, or binding in the linkage. If no problems are uncovered in these areas, replace the vacuum unit. Its diaphragm is probably ruptured.

3. Choke unloader operation. The choke

unloader is operated by the throttle and is placed on the choke to permit the driver to relieve a flooding condition by cranking the engine with the throttle held to the floor. The choke unloader mechanism forces the choke part-way open mechanically, to provide a leaner mixture than is usually required when the engine is cold.

The mechanism usually consists of a tang which is mounted on the end of the throttle shaft near the fast idle cam. When the throttle is opened wide, the tang bears against one side of the fast idle cam. The fast idle cam is mounted on a shaft which protrudes from the side of the carburetor body. A linkage connects the cam and a lever mounted on the end of the choke shaft. The effect is that the unloader tang turns the cam slightly, which in turn, through its linkage, forces the choke valve part-way open regardless of the pressure of the thermostatic spring.

The tang is usually bent to adjust the opening of the unloader. A drill of specified size is inserted between the edge of the choke flap and the carburetor throttle bore wall, the choke is forced gently closed, and the throttle is held wide open. The adjustment is correct when the tang is bent so the unloader mechanism just allows the choke flap to be closed until it contacts the drill. If specific instructions and specifications are not available, an ineffective unloader mechanism can be made more effective by gently bending the tang so the choke will be opened somewhat more.

4. Fast idle adjustment. The fast idle mechanism uses the choke linkage to position a cam, which, under cold conditions, moves under the engine idle adjustment screw or an auxiliary screw provided for fast cold idle. Either cold stalling or racing of the engine can usually be cured by bringing the fast idle adjustment to specifications. Fast idle is generally adjusted with the engine warm in order to standardize the conditions within the manifold and combustion chambers. The fast idle cam is manually turned to place the fast idle screw on the specified spot of the cam, for example, the highest point on the second step of the cam and the screw adjusted until the engine speed meets specifications (as measured by a tachometer).

Of course, adjustments can be made to cure either racing or cold stalling without the use of a tachometer and factory specs. However, such adjustments are frequently inadequate to cure the problem or else cause another problem, perhaps the opposite of the original. Specs and a tachometer allow a much more satisfactory adjustment.

G. Check for Carburetor Internal Problems.

NOTE: *A carburetor is an extremely delicate, precision instrument. Carburetor disassembly and work should be attempted only by someone familiar with carburetion, or at least experienced with general mechanics. If possible, a* Chilton Auto Repair Manual *or factory manual should be consulted so that disassembly can be accomplished without damage. Also, it is recommended, for safety's sake, that gasoline not be used as a solvent because of its flammability. Other solvents are available at auto parts stores.*

In all cases, a carburetor gasket kit should be purchased before disassembly to permit replacement of all the gaskets that are disturbed in the process of disassembly. Gaskets, in general, *cannot* be expected to survive such an operation intact.

If the problem is a stuck float or other, relatively minor, malfunction, treat the carburetor with a carburetor cleaning solvent. If the only cause of malfunction is dirt accumulation, the problem can frequently be solved by such a treatment, thus saving the time and trouble of disassembly. Persistent problems are probably the result of mechanical wear and disassembly will, therefore, be required.

Disassembly is usually accomplished as follows:

1. Remove the carburetor linkages and fuel line, and then remove the nuts which hold the unit to the manifold. Place the unit on a clean bench.

2. Remove all external linkages.

3. Remove the float bowl cover which is generally held on to the top of the carburetor with screws. The condition of the float, needle, and seat can usually be checked without further disassembly.

4. Remove the choke and float parts. Remove the power piston.

5. Remove the main jets, venturi cluster, and the throttle body from the bowl.

6. Disassemble the throttle body. Do

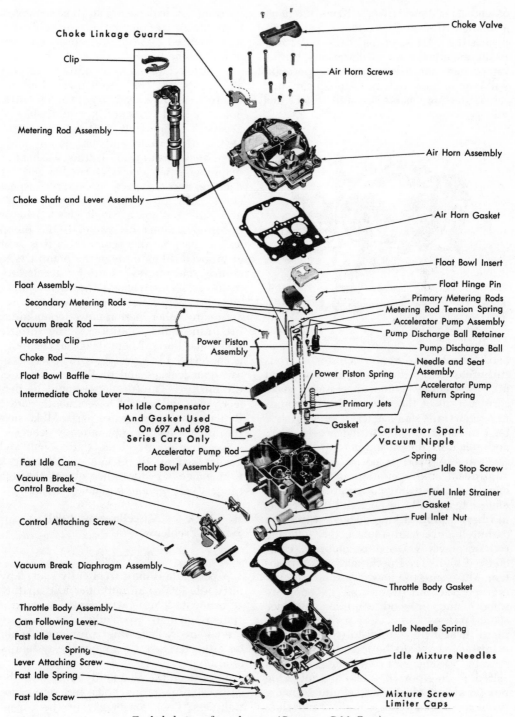

Choke Linkage Guard
Clip
Metering Rod Assembly
Choke Shaft and Lever Assembly
Choke Valve
Air Horn Screws
Air Horn Assembly
Air Horn Gasket
Float Bowl Insert
Float Assembly
Secondary Metering Rods
Vacuum Break Rod
Horseshoe Clip
Choke Rod
Float Bowl Baffle
Intermediate Choke Lever
Power Piston Assembly
Float Hinge Pin
Primary Metering Rods
Metering Rod Tension Spring
Accelerator Pump Assembly
Pump Discharge Ball Retainer
Pump Discharge Ball
Needle and Seat Assembly
Accelerator Pump Return Spring
Power Piston Spring
Primary Jets
Gasket
Hot Idle Compensator And Gasket Used On 697 And 698 Series Cars Only
Accelerator Pump Rod
Float Bowl Assembly
Fast Idle Cam
Vacuum Break Control Bracket
Control Attaching Screw
Vacuum Break Diaphragm Assembly
Carburetor Spark Vacuum Nipple
Spring
Idle Stop Screw
Fuel Inlet Strainer
Gasket
Fuel Inlet Nut
Throttle Body Gasket
Throttle Body Assembly
Cam Following Lever
Fast Idle Lever
Spring
Lever Attaching Screw
Fast Idle Spring
Fast Idle Screw
Idle Needle Spring
Idle Mixture Needles
Mixture Screw Limiter Caps

Exploded view of a carburetor (Courtesy, G.M. Corp)

not remove the idle mixture adjustment screws on late-model cars unless damage is evident.

Check the carburetor as outlined below:

a. Shake the float to make sure it is dry inside. If there is any evidence of fuel in-side, replace the float. Inspect the needle and seat for wear. If there is evidence of a groove in the needle, replace the needle and seat. Upon reassembling the float mechanism, make sure the float is aligned properly (so its edge is parallel to the edge of the float bowl cover). Bend the float arm slightly if an adjustment is necessary. Adjust the float level and drop according to the manufacturer's specifications. Ensuring proper float, needle, and seat operation will cure many problems of rough running, hard starting, flooding, and poor fuel mileage.

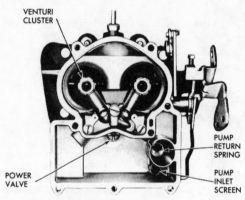

The venturi cluster (© G.M. Corp)

b. Mounting of venturi cluster. If your carburetor is not dirty or badly worn, and full disassembly is not necessary, make sure that all of the venturi cluster mounting screws are snug. A leaky venturi cluster can cause rough idle, flat acceleration, and generally rough running.

c. Metering rod or power system valve adjustment and condition of parts. The metering valves and power system valves cannot be visually inspected. If the vehicle has been run for a long distance without a carburetor overhaul, replace the metering rod or power valve rods and jets, especially if high-speed performance is a problem. Make sure the power piston or metering rod vacuum piston and its bore are smooth and in good condition. Replace scored pistons. Inspect any springs, and replace them if they are distorted or broken. Adjustments should be made during reassembly. Specific procedures must be consulted. Curing power system and metering rod problems will help to eliminate many problems of poor fuel economy and sluggish performance.

d. The appearance of the fuel in the float bowl will indicate whether or not clean fuel is being supplied to the carburetor. If evidence of dirt or water in the bowl exists, clean the fuel system or clean or replace filters and strainers as necessary. The float bowl should be carefully

checked for leakage while it is separated from the rest of the carburetor. This will be evidenced by a rapid drop in the level of fuel in the bowl.

e. Accelerator pump condition. Inspect all points in the mechanical linkages where wear may occur (e.g., shafts, bores, holes in shaft arms, etc.), and replace if necessary. Inspect all shaft arms for tightness on their shafts and replace any loose assemblies. Inspect any leather washers or diaphragms for cracks, turned edges, or damage, and replace as necessary. Inspect check balls for corrosion or other roughness, and replace a rough check ball or distorted retainer or spring. If the pump uses a check needle, replace it if it is bent or grooved. Blow through the pump jets to ensure cleanliness. Curing accelerator pump problems will aid throttle response and, in some cases, improve gas mileage and cure other performance complaints.

f. Inspect the condition of the throttle shafts and bores. About 0.005 in. clearance is normal. Excessively worn parts will cause air leakage and resultant dilution of the mixture. Throttle flaps should be perfectly flat and should have smooth edges. Replace excessively worn parts. Make sure the main jets (if not already checked under item c.) are clean. Use solvent and compressed air for cleaning, as forcing a thin gauge wire or other object through the jets will *invariably* damage them.

H. Check for Miscellaneous Fuel System Problems.

POOR IDLE

A poor idle is most frequently caused by dirty idle jets or an improper idle mixture adjustment. In cars with emission control systems, though, especially where mixture screws are sealed, other problems should be suspected first. Check out the system as follows:

1. Inspect the manifold bolts, and the carburetor mounting bolts and screws for tightness. Look for cracks in the carburetor body or warping, which would be indicated by unevenness in the seams between the various sections of the carburetor. Manifold leaks can be detected by pouring oil on the joints between the manifold and engine block while the engine is idling. Improvement in idle indicates leaks. Intake manifold bolts should be tightened

OH	VEHICLE EMISSION CONTROL INFORMATION	GM	C.C.S. EXHAUST EMISSION CONTROL	
455 CU. IN. 4 BBL. CARB.	OLDSMOBILE DIVISION GENERAL MOTORS CORP.		DWELL	30°
			TIMING (DEG. BTDC @ RPM)	10° @ 1100
			SPARK PLUGS GAP	.040°
			SPARK PLUGS TYPE	AC R 46S
			CARBURETOR SCREW(RPM)	600 (IN DRIVE)
			FAST IDLE SCREW(RPM)	1050 (IN PARK)
			CHOKE SETTING	INDEX

MAKE ADJUSTMENTS WITH ENGINE AT NORMAL OPERATING
TEMPERATURE, CHOKE OPEN AND AIR CONDITIONING OFF.
PLUG DISCONNECTED VACUUM FITTINGS.
    SET PARKING BRAKE AND BLOCK DRIVE WHEELS.
1. DISCONNECT CARBURETOR HOSE FROM VAPOR CANISTER.
2. DISCONNECT DISTR. VACUUM HOSE. PLUG HOSE TO CARB.
3. SET DWELL AND TIMING AT SPECIFIED RPM.
4. ADJUST CARBURETOR SPEED SCREW TO SPECIFIED RPM.
5. WITH TRANSMISSION IN PARK(OR NEUTRAL). SET FAST IDLE
   TO SPECIFIED RPM ON LOW STEP OF CAM.
6. RECONNECT DISTRIBUTOR AND CANISTER HOSES.

    FUEL REQUIREMENTS — USE 91 OCTANE OR HIGHER
SEE OLDSMOBILE SERVICE MANUAL FOR ADDITIONAL INFORMATION
THIS LABEL USED WITH ENGINE CODE: US-UT

IDLE MIXTURE PRESET AT FACTORY. DO NOT REMOVE CAPS.

THIS VEHICLE CONFORMS TO U.S. DEPT. OF H.E.W. AND CALIFORNIA REGULATIONS APPLICABLE TO 1971 MODEL YEAR NEW MOTOR VEHICLES.

A typical engine compartment emission control information sticker (© G.M. Corp)

to specifications using a torque wrench. Consult a manual for the specified torque and tightening pattern.

2. If the vehicle has adjustable mixture screws, adjust them for the fastest possible idle speed. A tachometer or vacuum gauge can be used to indicate highest idle speed or manifold vacuum. Follow the instructions on the engine compartment sticker for idle mixture adjustments if the vehicle was built to meet emission standards. Where idle mixture screws are capped, all other possibilities should be exhausted before removing the caps and adjusting the mixture.

3. Make sure the engine is idling at the specified idle speed. Too slow an idle can cause rough running. Use a tachometer and consult the engine compartment sticker or owner's manual for idle speed specifications.

4. Check the PCV system. Replace the PCV valve if pinching the PCV hose near the valve does not cause idle speed to drop 40–80 rpm. Inspect all hoses for bad connections, cracks, or breaks.

5. Check the thermostatically controlled air cleaner. The air cleaner flap should cut off all engine compartment air and draw all air through the heat stove until the engine and compartment are warm. The flap should then remain closed enough to maintain a temperature of 85° F in the air horn. If the flap does not seem to function properly, the system may be tested by placing a small thermometer in the air horn with the air cleaner assembled and the engine operating. Check all hoses and connections, inspect the linkage between the diaphragm and flap, and test the flap by applying 9 in. of vacuum directly through the supply hose. Replace the diaphragm or repair the linkage as necessary. If the diaphragm tests out to be all right, replace the heat sensor. Supply air at less than 85° F will cause rough idle in cars using air preheat systems because of the very lean idle mixtures used.

6. Check the condition of the spark plugs, ignition timing and dwell, and look for leaks in the vacuum advance lines and diaphragms if fuel system problems are not uncovered. If the carburetor's idle mixture screws are capped, follow the manufacturer's specific instructions for the vehicle so the adjustment will not adversely affect exhaust emissions.

VAPOR LOCK

1. Check for unusual climatic conditions. If the weather is unusually warm for the time of year, vapor lock may occur because the fuel was formulated for easy starting in cooler weather, and thus contains an excessive amount of volatile hydrocarbons for the conditions.

2. Check the routing of the fuel lines to make sure the lines do not touch or run close to a hot engine part. Relocate the lines as necessary.

3. Check for any source of excess heat such as poor ignition timing and dwell, clogged cooling system, or slipping belts. Check to see that the manifold heat control valve operates freely; free it with solvent if necessary.

4. Check to see that fuel pump output and pressure meet specifications, and that

the float system is in good condition and is properly adjusted.

5. If the problem persists in spite of the vehicle being in good mechanical condition, the manufacturer may provide a replacement fuel pump incorporating a vapor return line. Installation of such a kit will usually alleviate the problem.

STALLING

1. Check fast idle and regular idle adjustments and bring them to specifications.

2. If the engine stalls when cold, check the function and adjustment of the choke mechanism as in subsection F.

3. If the engine stalls when warmed up, check the float level and the condition of the float needle and seat as in G. Check fuel pump pressure to make sure it is not too high. Check for worn or loose gaskets that might cause carburetor air or fuel leaks. If an anti-stall dashpot is used, check it for a faulty vacuum hose, ruptured diaphragm, or bent mounting bracket.

4. If the engine stalls only when very hot, check the hot idle compensator if the carburetor has one. This is a thermostatic valve that provides extra air to the carburetor when the engine is idling at higher-than-normal temperatures. It compensates for the abnormal amount of fuel vapor generated under these conditions. The valve draws its air from inside the air horn. Block off this port with the engine idling hot. If there is no reduction in idle speed, the carburetor will have to be disassembled and the compensator checked according to the manufacturer's instructions. The cooling system and manifold heat control valve should also be checked.

RUNNING ON

1. Bring idle speed to specifications. If necessary, set idle with the idle stop solenoid energized and also with it de-energized.

2. Make sure that the throttle linkage allows the throttle to close fully. If the carburetor uses a solenoid to control idle speed, make sure that when the ignition switch is turned off, the solenoid permits the throttle to close so that the slow idle screw becomes effective. Replace a faulty solenoid.

3. Check for any source of excess heat. Check ignition timing, and the condition of the cooling system and manifold heat control valve, and then correct any defects. Check spark plug heat range.

4. If the problem persists, the combustion chambers are probably severely carboned. In some cases, the carbon can be removed by slowly pouring a solvent manufactured for decarbonizing the engine into the carburetor while the engine is idling.

NOTE: *Do not try to correct the problem by removing or changing the cooling system thermostat to a lower temperature unit as this will accelerate engine wear and increase exhaust emissions. In some systems, the thermostat blocks the radiator bypass during heavy load conditions. In these systems, removal can cause over heating.*

5 · Compression

What Compression Is

In the description of engine operation, it was mentioned that, after the closing of the intake valve, the air/fuel mixture is trapped in the cylinder as the piston rises. The volume of the combustion chamber after the piston reaches TDC is about $\frac{1}{8}$th to $\frac{1}{11}$th of the volume of the whole cylinder. Compressing the mixture in this manner raises the pressures and temperatures in the combustion chambers during the power stroke, thus improving combustion and increasing the amount of power delivered to the piston on the downstroke.

Any leakage in the combustion chamber will reduce the pressure created during the compression stroke. The pressure created in the combustion chamber may be measured with a gauge that remains at the highest reading it measures, through the action of a one-way valve. This gauge is inserted into the spark plug hole. A compression test will uncover many mechanical problems that can cause rough running or poor performance.

Positioning the gauge in the spark plug hole (© G.M. Corp)

Compression Testing and Troubleshooting

A. Prepare the engine for the test as follows:

1. Operate the engine until it reaches operating temperature. The engine is at operating temperature a few minutes after hot water begins circulating through both radiator hoses.

2. Remove the primary lead from the positive terminal on the coil. Remove all high-tension wires from the spark plugs.

3. Clean all dirt and foreign material from around the spark plugs (compressed air works well) and remove all spark plugs.

4. If a remote starter switch is available, hook it up according to its manufacturer's instructions.

5. Remove the air cleaner and block or wire the throttle and choke in the wide open position. The secondary bores may be ignored on four-barrel carburetors.

B. Zero the gauge, place it firmly in one of the spark plug holes, and crank the engine for about five compression strokes. Record the reading and the number or position of the cylinder tested. *Release pressure from the gauge.*

C. Repeat the test for all the other cylinders.

D. Evaluate the results. Consult a manual for the compression pressure rating of the engine. Engines with compression ratios of 8:1–8.5:1 usually produce 140–150 lbs pressure. Higher compression ratios produce up to 175 lbs. The readings should be within 25 percent of each other. (See chart.)

If the test had to be performed on a cold engine because it could not be started, the readings will be considerably lower than normal, even if the engine is in perfect me-

Minimum and Maximum Compression Readings

Max. Press. Lbs. Sq. In.	Min. Press. Lbs. Sq. In.	Max. Press. Lbs. Sq. In.	Min. Press. Lbs. Sq. In.
134	101	188	141
136	102	190	142
138	104	192	144
140	105	194	145
142	107	196	147
146	110	198	148
148	111	200	150
150	113	202	151
152	114	204	153
154	115	206	154
156	117	208	156
158	118	210	157
160	120	212	158
162	121	214	160
164	123	216	162
166	124	218	163
168	126	220	165
170	127	222	166
172	129	224	168
174	131	226	169
176	132	228	171
178	133	230	172
180	135	232	174
182	136	234	175
184	138	236	177
186	140	238	178

chanical condition. A substantial pressure should still be produced, and variations in the readings are still indicative of the condition of the engine. If all readings are acceptable, see F.

E. Perform a "wet" compression test if any or all of the cylinders read low. Pour about one teaspoon of engine oil in each of the cylinders with low compression and repeat the test for each cylinder in turn.

F. Further evaluate the results. One or more of the symptoms below should apply:

1. All cylinders fall within the specified range of pressures. The engine internal parts are in generally good condition.

2. One or more cylinders produced a low reading in D. which was substantially improved by the "wet" compression test. Those cylinders have worn pistons, piston rings, and/or cylinder bores.

3. Two adjacent cylinders (or several pairs whose cylinders are adjacent) have nearly identical low readings, and did not respond to the "wet" compression test. These cylinders share leaks in the head gasket. This may be cross-checked by performing the cooling system pressure tests in the cooling system section, and by looking at the oil on the dipstick to see if coolant bubbles are present.

4. Compression buildup in one or more cylinders is erratic—it climbs less on some strokes than on others. Normally, the pressure rises steadily and then levels off. This indicates sticking valves. This problem may be cross-checked with a timing light. Remove the valve covers. Since this test is run with the engine operating and the valve covers removed, it would be wise to purchase and install special clips that are designed to stop oil flow to the valve train. Connect a timing light to the spark plug lead of the cylinder suspected of having sticky valves. Aim the timing light at the valves of the cylinder in question. Loosen the distributor and then start the engine and watch the valves. Vary the timing slightly, smoothly, and gradually in order to observe the position of the valve at slightly different points in the rotation of the engine. If there is an erratic motion of either valve, that valve is sticking. Remember to retime the ignition system and remove the oil clips.

6 · The Cooling System

How It Works

The cooling system, in spite of its compact size, handles a staggering amount of heat in order to protect the internal parts of the engine from the heat of combustion and friction. The cooling system of a modern car may remove about 6,000 BTU per minute, or considerably more heat than is required to comfortably warm a large home in extreme weather.

The coolant employed now is generally a mixture of water and ethylene glycol. Ethylene glycol is a chemical which, when mixed with water in the proper proportions, both lowers the freezing point and raises the boiling point of the solution.

Most commercial antifreezes also contain additives designed to inhibit corrosion and foaming in the system.

The water pump is the heart of the cooling system. This is usually driven off the pulley on the front of the engine crankshaft by V belts. Its bearings are usually sealed ball bearing units located in the long snout of the front pump housing. The pump's impeller is a vaned wheel which fits the inside of the water pump housing with a very close clearance. Water trapped between the vanes is forced to rotate with the impeller around the inside of the water pump housing. The resultant centrifugal force raises the pressure in the pump discharge, causing water to flow through the pump.

The coolant is discharged into the front

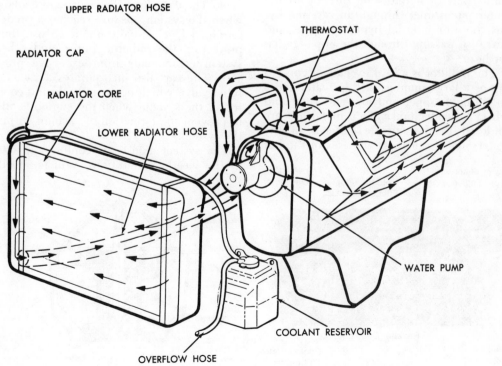

UPPER RADIATOR HOSE

THERMOSTAT

RADIATOR CAP

RADIATOR CORE

LOWER RADIATOR HOSE

WATER PUMP

COOLANT RESERVOIR

OVERFLOW HOSE

The flow of coolant through a typical V8 engine (© G.M. Corp)

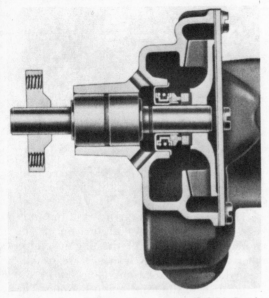

Cross-section of a typical water pump (© G.M. Corp)

of the engine block and circulates in the water jackets around the cylinders. It then makes its way upward through ports in the block, head gasket, and head to the water passages around the combustion chambers. It leaves the engine through the front of the block, passing into the thermostat housing which, in V8 engines, is a part of the intake manifold. Here, the water flow splits; part of it returning directly to the water pump inlet through an external by-pass hose or internal bypass passage, and part of it passing through the upper radiator hose.

The radiator is a heat exchanger consisting of a large number of thin water tubes fed through upper and lower or right and left side header tanks. Thin metal fins are soldered to the outside surfaces of the water tubes to increase the area of the hot

metal surfaces available for transmission of heat to the air. A fan, usually driven off the water pump shaft, aids circulation of air through the radiator, especially at low speeds. Some fans have a thermostatically operated fluid drive clutch to adjust the fan speed to temperature conditions and engine speed.

A heater core, similar in construction to the radiator, receives coolant flow from the lower portion of the thermostat housing where coolant flows at all times. The heater hoses conduct the water to the core and return it to the inlet side of the water pump. The heater core is usually in a heater air duct located in the dash panel.

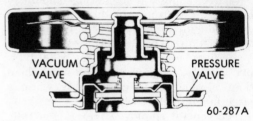

Cross-section of a radiator cap (© G.M. Corp)

A pressure cap seals the radiator against coolant leakage through the action of a sprung poppet valve whose rubber sealing ring bears against a surface inside the filler neck. The cap allows the escape of coolant when the system pressure reaches a predetermined level, usually about 15 psi, thus protecting the radiator, hoses, and other system components from excessive pressure. The cap also incorporates a vacuum relief valve which opens only during cooling of the system (when the engine is off) to prevent the formation of vacuum within the system.

The system adjusts its cooling capacity to the weather conditions, vehicle speed,

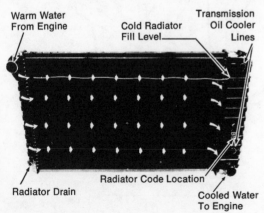

A typical cross-flow radiator (© G.M. Corp)

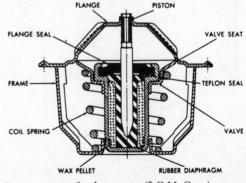

Cross-section of a thermostat (© G.M. Corp)

and engine load through the action of a thermostat. The thermostat consists of a poppet or hinged flap type of valve actuated by pressure from a fluid-filled bellows or wax pellet. The valve remains tightly closed below the rated opening temperature, forcing all the coolant discharged from the water pump to return directly to the water pump inlet. This practically eliminates loss of heat from the engine during warm-up, while protecting the system from the formation of steam at hot spots. The bypass inlet is situated near the heat-sensing portion of the thermostat so the thermostat will receive a continuous indication of the water temperature, even when none of the fluid is passing through it.

When coolant temperature reaches the specified level (usually 180–195°), the thermostat will begin opening. The valve will be opened gradually as coolant temperatures rise, and will reach a wide-open position about 25° above the opening temperature. The radiator is slightly larger than required during most operating conditions. Thus, the thermostat is usually at least part-way closed, providing a precise control of engine temperature. One exception is when the engine is idled or turned off immediately after a hard run. The cooling system's capacity to throw off heat is vastly decreased under these conditions but the great amount of heat stored up in the heavy metal of the engine block continues to warm the coolant. It is normal for the engine temperature to rise substantially under these conditions. As long as water is not discharged from the pressure cap, there is nothing wrong with the system.

RUST AND SCALE

Rust and scale cause engine cooling problems in two different ways. First, they restrict the flow of coolant which decreases the flow through the entire system. Second, they build up a layer of insulating material on all the surfaces of the system. This not only reduces the capacity of the system to throw off heat but also keeps the coolant from picking up heat in the normal manner from hot engine parts even when the coolant is running at near normal temperatures.

Rust and scale are a result of chemical reactions between the metals in the cooling system and the minute amounts of air and exhaust gases that always enter the system through the water pump shaft seal and the head gasket and the block and head. Rust and scale cause what is perhaps the most common problem in poorly maintained systems, and can cause severe overheating even when there are no leaks in the system and the engine is in good mechanical condition.

Quick Reference Guide For Cooling System Troubleshooting

A. *Inspect the system.* Check the fan and drive belt(s), coolant (level and condition) and the cap. Check for leaks. Check for operating conditions that are more severe than those for which the vehicle was designed. Check for an indication of overheating on the gauge or as indicated by the warning light. Check the thermostat. Check the circulation and listen to the water pump for excessive noise. Check the ignition timing, resetting it as necessary.

B. *Check the radiator cap with a pressure tester.*

C. *Use a radiator pressure tester to test the system's ability to hold pressure.* Check for head gasket leaks by idling the engine with the system pressurized. Test compression if necessary.

D. *Check further for leaks, keeping the system pressurized.*

E. *Check the strength of the antifreeze solution.* Most modern systems require protection to 0° to ensure protection against corrosion and boiling.

F. *Remove the thermostat and test it for proper operation.*

G. *Check the wiring to the temperature light or gauge. Replace parts as necessary.*

Cooling System Troubleshooting

A. Inspect the System.

Check the fan for bent, cracked, or broken blades and replace it as necessary. A thermostatic fan may be checked as follows:

1. Allow the engine to cool until the engine compartment is well below 150° F.

2. Cover the radiator, leaving sufficient room for circulation so air will flow through the core and fan in the normal direction.

3. Measure the temperature of the fan air discharge with a 200° F thermometer. There should be a sudden increase in noise produced by the fan between 150 and 190° F. Otherwise the unit is faulty and should be replaced.

Check the belts that drive the water pump for cracks and glazing, and replace as necessary.

NOTE: *Replace paired belts with a set, even if one looks serviceable. Use the proper size. Do not pry the belt on. Tighten to specifications.*

Adjusting belt tension with a strand tension gauge (Courtesy, Chrysler Corp)

Check the belt tension and adjust it to specifications if a strand tensioning gauge is available. If not, adjust the belt so that tension exists on it at all times, and heavy thumb pressure will permit it to flex about ½ in. Tighten a new belt just a bit more snugly to allow for the tension that will be lost as the belt adapts to the pulley grooves during the first few miles of operation.

Make sure that the engine has had time to cool down, and remove the radiator cap to check the condition of the coolant.

NOTE: *Unless the engine is cold, use a heavy rag to do this. Turn the cap very slowly, pausing to allow pressure to escape.*

The coolant level should be 1–2 in. below the filler neck if the engine is warm, and about 3 in. if it is cold. If the coolant level is low, start the engine and allow it to idle while adding a 50 percent antifreeze, 50 percent water solution to the radiator.

Check the condition of the coolant. It should be clear. If there is evidence of rust and scale and the coolant is dull brown or rusty red, flush the system because clogging and poor heat transfer are probably contributing to the problem.

Check the seal in the radiator cap for cracks or torn sections. Replace it if the seal is cracked, torn or hangs out over the edges of the metal backing.

Check the radiator and hoses, especially the hose connections, for rust marks that would indicate leakage. Tighten clamps or replace hoses and clamps as necessary.

In order to conserve weight and space, most modern cooling systems are carefully sized to provide just the capacity required under normal operating conditions. If the vehicle is being used to pull a trailer that weighs more than one ton, overheating problems are probably due to the load. Installation of a trailer towing package will probably cure the problem. If the vehicle has an aftermarket air conditioner, overheating is probably due to the extra resistance to air flow, engine load, and heat produced by the unit. Install a heavy-duty radiator and fan. Finally, if your vehicle overheats during prolonged idling with the air conditioning running and the automatic transmission in gear, a change in operating habits may cure the problem. The transmission should be shifted to neutral during such idling. The heat generated in the transmission under idling conditions is passed on to a transmission oil cooler located in the radiator. Under extreme conditions, the idle speed should be increased with the throttle and the air conditioning should be turned off. Overheating should not be considered a problem unless the vehicle has trouble cooling itself under normal road operating conditions.

Allow the engine to cool until it is well below normal operating temperature. Start the engine and operate it at fast idle. The radiator should remain fairly cool for a few minutes and then suddenly turn warm. Coolant should flow through the entire radiator and both hoses, making them warm to the touch. Scattered cool spots in the radiator mean clogging. Failure of the coolant to circulate through the lower hose may mean a faulty water pump or thermostat, or severe clogging. Slow warm-up of the engine and circulation of only moderately warm water through the radiator immediately after starting means a bad thermostat that might be causing overheating.

Accelerate the engine to check to see if the radiator's lower hose collapses at higher speeds. If it does, replace it. Listen to the water pump. A loud grinding noise usually indicates worn bearings and contact between the impeller blades and water pump housing because of the improper bearing clearances. Replace a noisy pump.

Road-test the vehicle, watching the temperature gauge or light, and stopping frequently to check for coolant loss from the overflow tube.

If the gauge or light indicates overheating, and water is expelled through the overflow tube, follow through with the rest of the checks in the suggested order. If the gauge indicates overheating but there is no evidence of coolant loss, see B. If the radiator cap checks out, go on to G. If the only problem is expulsion of coolant through the overflow, with no other signs of overheating, see B. If the radiator cap checks out, go to subsection E. If the only problem is slow warm-up, replace the thermostat.

Testing the radiator cap (© G.M. Corp)

Adjust the ignition timing to specifications. Improper timing can result in overheating by reducing the efficiency of the engine.

B. Check the Radiator Pressure Cap with a Pressure Tester.

A special tester with an air pump is available for this purpose. It is the only way to adequately test a pressure cap. Check the pressure rating of the cap (which is usually stamped on the top), wet the rubber seal, and install the cap onto the tester. Pump up the pressure tester until air bleeds out from under the seal. Note the pressure. It should be within one pound of the rating on the cap. Replace the cap if pressure is released at either too high or too low a pressure; a cap which retains excess pressure can damage the system and can also make removel of the cap dangerous.

Testing the ability of the system to hold pressure (Courtesy, American Motors)

C. Use a Radiator Pressure Tester to Test the System's Ability to Hold Pressure.

Pressurize the system up to the rating of the cap. Carefully watch the pressure gauge for several minutes to see if there is a loss of pressure. If there is no pressure loss, go on to E. If pressure is lost, idle the engine and watch the gauge carefully for fluctuations. Be sure to release pressure if there is a continuous rise after starting the engine. If there are no fluctuations but there is a slow pressure loss, proceed to D. Otherwise, remove the spark plug leads one by one to determine which cylinders are leaking. The leaking cylinder(s) will produce less fluctuation in the needle when the spark leads are removed. If obvious differences between cylinders are not noted in this test, perform a compression test as described in the previous section. Leaky cylinders must be repaired by removing the cylinder head(s) affected and replacing the head gasket.

D. Check Further for Leaks, Keeping the System Pressurized.

Keep the pressure in the system to within a pound or two of the full rating. This will cause leaks to show up that only exist under full operating pressure. Check the following parts of the system very carefully: hoses, radiator (especially at soldered joints between header tanks and water tubes), water pump (especially at the shaft seal), thermostat housing, heater core (check the floor in the passenger compartment for a light film of antifreeze), drain cocks and plugs, core plugs in block, and heater water valves (especially around valve stems). Replace any defective parts.

E. Check Strength of Antifreeze Solution.

Regardless of the climate, a modern, high-pressure system should be protected down to 0° F because ethylene-glycol antifreeze in solution with water increases the boiling point. Even with all other cooling system components in perfect condition, a weak antifreeze solution could result in boiling of coolant under difficult operating conditions.

Make the test using a special hydrometer calibrated to show the freezing point of an ethylene-glycol and water solution. Pull the solution in and out of the hydrometer several times to make sure that any residue from the last test is removed and to bring the thermometer in the hydrometer to the temperature of the solution as quickly as possible. If the unit does not have a thermometer and is not equipped

with a temperature conversion chart, a sample of coolant will have to be brought to the temperature at which the unit is calibrated to obtain an accurate reading.

The test must either be performed at the specified temperature or corrected with a conversion chart because a change in temperature will affect the reading by changing the density of the sample. If there is not adequate protection, consult an antifreeze chart, drain the coolant, and replace it with the correct antifreeze solution. Be sure to retest the new solution to ensure adequate protection.

F. Remove the Thermostat and Test It for Proper Operation.

Secure a new thermostat housing gasket before proceeding with this test, as disassembly of the housing usually ruins the old gasket. Drain coolant from the radiator down below the level of the thermostat housing. Remove the thermostat and notice whether or not the wax pellet or bellows was turned downward, toward the block. A thermostat that is upside down will respond improperly to temperature changes.

Suspend the thermostat in a pan full of water, keeping it well above the bottom so that heat will not be conducted directly to the sensing element from the bottom of the pan. Place the pan on a stove and heat it while measuring the water temperature with a 250° thermometer. The thermostat should open within 5° of its rated opening temperature (consult the owner's manual for the rating), and open fully about 25° above this temperature. (These conditions cannot be created for a 195° thermostat, but a check of opening temperature and freedom of operation can be made.) After proper opening and freedom of operation have been checked, allow the solution to cool and make sure that the thermostat closes properly.

Replace the thermostat, if necessary. In reassembly, make sure that the wax pellet or bellows is downward (toward the main portion of the block). Clean the surfaces between the upper and lower portions of the housing and replace the gasket.

If problems continue, remove the external bypass hose, if one is used, and inspect it for clogging or swelling. Replace it if it does not permit free passage of coolant.

G. Check Wiring-to-Temperature Light or Gauge. Replace Parts as Necessary.

Sometimes temperature gauges or lights will indicate overheating when there is no loss of coolant, or will fail to show overheating when coolant is lost. Failure to indicate overheating even when coolant is being lost through the overflow tube can occur because of a bad radiator cap or weak antifreeze solution. A bad sensor can cause the light or gauge to show overheating even when no problem exists.

A preliminary check of the wiring should be made in either case. Check the connection at the sensor, which is usually located in the cylinder head, to make sure it is clean and tight. Check the wiring for frayed insulation and grounds, and replace or repair it as necessary. Check the other dash gauges for normal function and, if they function normally, proceed with the checks below. If the other gauges do not work properly, there is an electrical system problem which should be rectified before blaming the cooling system gauge.

If the system pushes water out through the overflow tube, check the antifreeze solution as in subsection E. and correct a weak solution. Check the radiator pressure cap. A weak cap could cause coolant to escape even when the engine is not overheating. A cap that traps too much pressure can allow the engine to overheat without loss of coolant.

If the problem is not corrected, replace the sensor in the block. This is by far the most common source of trouble. If this does not rectify the problem, see the section on dash gauges and indicators.

Air Cooling Systems

Air cooling systems are generally trouble-free. A few problems can occur, however. If an air-cooled engine operates sluggishly after a short period of driving in warm weather, make the following checks:

A. Check the belt for glazing and cracks. If evidence of slippage exists, remove the belt to check the fan for free rotation and then replace the belt, tightening it to specifications to ensure adequate cooling.

B. Check all ducting for loose or missing screws or bent parts which might cause cracks and leaks. Check the spark plugs' rubber seals and heater hoses and clamps, and replace any parts which do not seal properly.

C. Check the ignition timing and, if applicable, the adjustment of the valves; poor tuning can cause high operating temperatures. Make sure the engine is using the right viscosity of motor oil.

D. If problems persist, check compression and check the oil pressure relief valve for proper spring tension and free plunger operation. Make repairs as necessary.

E. If the problem is still not solved, it may be necessary to remove the ducting and clean the entire engine of accumulated dirt. An oil cooler that is clogged internally can also cause overheating problems because of the importance of the oil as a coolant in an air-cooled engine. If there is evidence of sludge in the engine, it should be removed and cleaned. Check the operation and mounting of the thermostat. The thermostat should be wide open when the engine is idling after a hard run. The operation of the cooling flaps may be checked by disconnecting the bellows from the housing, and moving it back and forth to each of the extremes of the travel of the mechanism. Make sure that the mounting bracket is positioned so the bellows can fully open the cooling flaps.

7·Poor Engine Performance

Troubleshooting When The Engine Runs Poorly

When the engine refuses to start, the starting, ignition, and fuel systems, and the engine compression, should be checked as described in the preceding sections. When a minor operating problem exists, however, it frequently involves a small malfunction in one or several of the areas outlined in the preceding sections. Making a complete check of each of these aspects of engine operation would be unnecessarily time-consuming because the symptoms frequently offer clues as to the nature of the problem. Checking the appearance of the spark plugs and using a vacuum gauge will frequently reveal the nature of the problem very quickly.

This section describes how to evaluate spark plug appearance and vacuum gauge readings and contains various charts which will act as guides to using the material of the first four sections most effectively. If the engine generally runs roughly and performs poorly, carefully check the spark plugs and manifold vacuum before going to the charts. If a very minor and specific problem (e.g., hesitation on acceleration) exists, the charts should be consulted first.

It is for this type of troubleshooting that a general understanding of the operating principles of the various parts is important. For example, if a very rapid, regular misfiring occurs, it is obvious that the problem is confined to one cylinder, and that those parts which serve all the cylinders (such as the ignition points) are not at fault. If the engine runs acceptably when warmed up but refuses to start when cold, the choke is probably at fault. Keep the basic principles in mind while doing this kind of troubleshooting and you will save much time and labor.

SPARK PLUG EVALUATION

Begin this check by driving the car for several miles at reasonably high road speeds to thoroughly warm the engine. Stop the engine, clean around the plugs, remove the wires, and remove all spark plugs, keeping them in order so that, if serious problems are uncovered, the cylinders affected can be identified.

The chart below describes the appearance of the plugs and the indicated problems.

Appearance	Problem
Electrodes slightly eroded, light brown deposits. Gray or tan, glazed cinder-like lead deposits may be noticeable. Gap slightly wider than specified.	Normal wear.

Normal

Carbon fouling—dry, black, fluffy deposits.

Carbon fouled

On just one or two cylinders, this may indicate faulty high-tension leads or valve problems. If the problem is demonstrated on all cylinders, the fuel mixture may be too rich or the heat riser may not be functioning properly.

Oil fouling—wet black deposits.

Oil fouled

Piston rings, valve guides, or valve seals may be worn. The condition is normal on new or recently overhauled engines.

Gap bridging—heavy deposits lodged between the two electrodes.

Gap bridged

Transfer of deposits from the combustion chamber due to a sudden change in operating conditions. The plug(s) must be replaced.

Overheating—the electrodes will be burned, and the insulator will be extremely white in color and may show small black spots.

Excessive ignition advance, lean mixture, or insufficient installation torque.

Overheated

Preignition—severely burnt or melted electrodes, blistered or cracked insulator.

Melted

Plug heat range too hot, excessive ignition advance, insufficient spark plug installation torque, fuel mixture too lean, very poor compression, or fuel octane rating too low.

INTAKE MANIFOLD VACUUM TEST

Bring the engine to operating temperature. Install a vacuum guage in the intake manifold below the throttle plate. In older cars, there is usually a plugged port in the intake manifold. In newer cars, this port is used for the PCV system. Remove the plug or PCV hose from the valve and install the gauge line. Start the engine and allow it to idle. Gauge readings and their meanings are listed below:

Reading	Meaning
1. Steady, 17–22 in.	Normal reading.

Steady, from 17–22 in. Hg.

2. Low and steady, 10–15 in.	Late ignition timing, late valve timing, or uniformly low compression.

Low and steady

3. Very low, 5–10 in.	Vacuum leak.

Very low

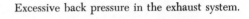

4. Regular fluctuation as engine speed is increased.

Ignition miss, or severe compression leak—usually caused by a valve or head gasket problem.

Needle fluctuates as engine speed increases

5. Gradual drop in the reading at idle just after engine is started.

Excessive back pressure in the exhaust system.

Gradual drop in reading at idle

6. Regular fluctuation at idle speed.

Ignition miss or sticking valve.

Intermittent fluctuation at idle

7. Steadily drifting needle.

Rich idle mixture or improperly synchronized dual carburetors.

Drifting needle

8. Needle drifts around, but in a noticeably irregular manner.

Lean mixture due to improper idle mixture adjustment or intake manifold or valve guide leakage.

9. Reading steady but too high (about 25 in.).

Ignition timing too far advanced.

High and steady

ENGINE TROUBLESHOOTING CHART

This troubleshooting chart will help guide you to effective use of the "Ignition System," "Fuel System," "Compression," and "Tune-up" sections of this book for the solution of the most common of the minor engine problems that occur. Consult the chart which most nearly fits the symptoms and, if necessary, see the appropriate section to eliminate each possible cause of trouble.

Engine Troubleshooting Chart

Engine runs well, but is hard to start when cold.

√ Improper oil viscosity. Use the recommended viscosity for the prevailing temperature.

√ Choke sticks due to gum on shafts or because of a bent shaft or link.

√ Choke is improperly adjusted.

√ Ignition coil, or high-tension wires are weak, or spark plug gap is too wide.

√ Moisture shorting out ignition components. Check for frayed insulation or a cracked distributor cap. If necessary, spray with a sealing compound.

√ Ignition timing and dwell improperly adjusted.

√ Fuel pump volume and pressure inadequate, or fuel lines or strainer partially clogged.

Engine misfires at high speeds only.

√ Spark plug gaps set too wide.

√ Improper dwell angle.

√ Weak ignition coil or high-tension wires.

√ Clogged fuel filter or strainer.

√ Inadequate fuel pump pressure or volume. (Volume should be 1 pt in 30–45 seconds)

Engine idles poorly or stalls.

√ Engine idle speed or mixture improperly adjusted.

√ Carburetor jets clogged.

√ Air leak at carburetor mounting, in intake manifold, or PCV system, or other vacuum hoses.

√ Incorrect valve clearance.

√ Clogged PCV valve or hose.

√ Stuck choke, improperly adjusted choke, or improper fast idle adjustment.

√ Faulty ignition components, incorrect timing and dwell, fouled spark plugs.

√ Poor compression or badly worn valves, camshaft, or camshaft drive.

Engine misses at various speeds.

√ Water or other foreign material in fuel.

√ Clogged carburetor jets.

√ Incorrect float level.

√ Improper spring tension on points or worn or loose distributor shaft or cam.

√ Insufficient dwell angle, or late ignition timing.

√ Weak coil or condenser.

√ Weak valve spring.

Engine Troubleshooting Chart-*Continued*

Engine lacks power.

√ Improper ignition timing.

√ Improper carburetor float level.

√ Fuel pump pressure and volume inadequate.

√ Distributor shaft and bushings worn.

√ Spark plugs dirty or improperly gapped.

√ Dwell angle incorrectly adjusted.

√ Weak coil or condenser.

√ Improper valve adjustment.

√ Poor compression.

√ Ignition advance diaphragm or hose leaking.

Oil consumption.

√ Oil of too light a viscosity or oil level too high.

√ Engine overheating.

√ External leaks at fuel pump, oil pan, timing chain cover, valve covers, rear seal.

√ Valve seals worn or damaged.

√ Worn valve stems or guides.

√ Excessive bearing clearance.

√ Worn cylinder walls, rings, or ring grooves.

√ Plugged cylinder head drainback holes.

Engine detonates (pings).

√ Ignition timing too far advanced.

√ Spark plugs of too high a heat range in use.

√ Manifold heat control valve stuck open.

√ Excessive carbon deposits in combustion chambers.

√ Improper fuel in use.

Engine hesitates on acceleration.

√ Ignition timing improperly set.

√ Accelerator pump circuit dirty, or inoperative due to mechanical problems.

√ Float level too low.

√ Inadequate fuel pump pressure and volume. (Volume should be 1 pt in 30–45 seconds.)

√ Accelerator pump jets not directed properly.

Engine valves noisy.

√ Improper adjustment. (See "Tune-up" section.)

√ Incorrect engine oil level.

√ Air leaks in oil pick-up.

√ Worn or clogged hydraulic lifters.

NOTE: *The faulty lifter(s) may be located by using a stethoscope to listen for noise while the engine is idling—with the valve cover(s) removed.*

√ Wear or breakage in valve train.

8 · The Tune-Up

Engine tune-ups are performed periodically to ensure continuous peak performance. They consist of various minor mechanical adjustments and inspection and/or replacement of perishable ignition system parts.

Tune-Up Procedures

1. Test Compression.

Compression testing can reveal mechanical problems which will not be corrected by a tune-up. A careful mechanic does a compression check as the first step in a tune-up to eliminate the possibility of internal malfunctions as the cause of poor performance.

Perform a compression test as described in the section on compression. When removing spark plugs, remember to clean the area around them before removal, and to place the plugs on a workbench, in order.

2. Service the Spark Plugs.

Manufacturers generally recommend replacement of spark plugs every 12,000 miles. Replace the plugs, if necessary, with plugs of the proper heat range.

If the plugs are to be reused:

a. Inspect the electrodes for burning and check the insulators for cracks. Replace any faulty plugs.

b. Clean the electrodes with a wire brush or, if possible, sandblast them. File the center electrodes flat, and regap the spark plugs to the specified gap. (Consult a Chilton's manual or factory manual for the specified gap.) Use a wire feeler gauge to set the gap. Bend the side electrode with a spark plug tool to change the gap.

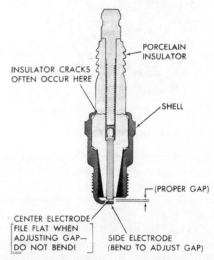

Where to measure spark plug gap (© G.M. Corp)

c. Make sure that all plugs are of the proper heat range, as specified by the manufacturer. (Consult the manual for heat range.)

NOTE: *Check the gaps on new plugs, even though some are pregapped. The gap has a great effect on engine performance.*

3. Replace the Plugs.

Use new gaskets on old plugs. Placing a drop of engine oil on the plug threads may help to ensure easy installation. *If possible, tighten the plugs with a torque wrench.* Inadequate torque causes spark plug burning, while excessive torque causes improper gap or damage to the cylinder head. All 10 mm spark plugs should be torqued to 14 ft lbs in a cast iron head, 11 ft lbs in an aluminum head. All 14 mm plugs (the most common size) should be torqued to 30 ft lbs in a cast iron head; 27 ft lbs in an aluminum head.

4. Service the Ignition Points.

Ignition points are usually replaced at 12,000 mile intervals with the spark plugs.

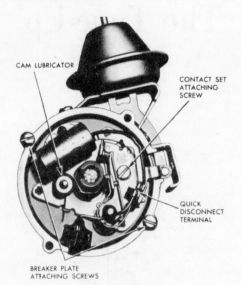

CAM LUBRICATOR

CONTACT SET
ATTACHING
SCREW

QUICK
DISCONNECT
TERMINAL

BREAKER PLATE
ATTACHING SCREWS

A typical contact set (© G.M. Corp)

The condenser is usually replaced as well. If the points are not severely burned or pitted, however, they may be reused. Used points should be removed, cleaned with a point file, and replaced.

> NOTE: *This operation is performed only to remove excess carbon deposits from the points. Do not attempt to remove all roughness on the contact surfaces, or else their special, wear-resistant coating may be destroyed.*

Lubricate the cam follower with a small dab of high-melting-point grease. If the distributor uses a cam lubricator, rotate it or replace it as the manufacturer recommends. Clean all old grease from the distributor cam before reinstalling or replacing the points.

5. Adjust the Point Gap or Dwell Angle.

If a dwell meter is available, it should be used for adjusting the dwell angle. This method is more accurate than gapping the points.

a. Gapping the points. This is a good method of making a preliminary setting of the dwell angle even if a dwell meter is available. Install the points (and condenser, if it is being replaced), ensuring that all connections are pushed on or screwed together securely and, if the condenser is being replaced, that it is securely mounted to ensure a good ground. If the mounting screw on the ignition points assembly is also used to make the gap adjustment, tighten it just enough to hold the

contacts apart. Rotate the engine until the tip of one of the distributor cams sits squarely under the cam follower on the movable contact arm. Using a leaf type feeler gauge (gap the points as specified in the manual), move the base plate of the point assembly back and forth until the gauge just slips between the two contacts when it is forced straight through. If the mounting screw serves as the adjusting lock, the contact assembly may usually be moved by wedging a screwdriver blade between a slot in the contact base plate and a protrusion on the surface of the distributor plate. In assemblies with an adjusting screw which is accessible from outside the distributor, an allen wrench is inserted into the head of the adjusting screw and rotated to make the adjustment. When the points are pitted, make sure the gauge does not come in contact with the built-up portion on one of the contact surfaces. A wire feeler gauge may help to make the most accurate adjustment when the points are pitted.

> NOTE: *Make sure all gauges are clean in gapping the points. An oily gauge will cause rapid point burning.*

b. Setting dwell angle. Connect the positive lead of the dwell meter to the distributor side of the coil, and the negative lead to a good ground. Make sure all wires are clear of moving parts and then start the engine. Run the engine at normal idle speed with the transmission in gear if the vehicle is equipped with an automatic

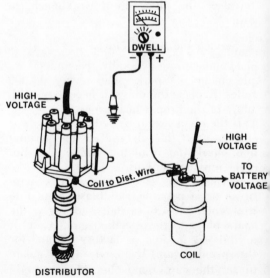

HIGH
VOLTAGE

DWELL

HIGH
VOLTAGE

TO
BATTERY
VOLTAGE

Coil to Dist. Wire

COIL

DISTRIBUTOR

Setting the dwell angle

transmission. Switch the dwell meter to the appropriate scale, according to the instructions on the dial. If the dwell is not within the range specified on the engine compartment sticker or in the manual, make the point gap narrower to increase the dwell angle, or wider to decrease it, until it falls within the specified range. If the vehicle has an automatic transmission, place it in Park. Accelerate the engine to about 2,000 rpm and watch the dwell angle. There should be very little variation in the dwell if the distributor is in good condition. If the dwell indicator moves about considerably, the distributor shaft and bushings may be badly worn. Some late-model distributors vary the dwell slightly to control emissions. However, this effect would be gradual and smooth, as contrasted with the erratic variation indicative of badly worn distributor parts.

6. Inspect the Secondary Ignition Circuit.

Inspect the inside surface of the distributor cap for cracks, carbon tracks, or badly burned contacts. To remove carbon tracks, wash the cap in soap and water and dry thoroughly. Replace the cap if it is cracked or if the contacts are badly eroded.

Inspect the rotor for cracks, excessive burning of the contacts, and mechanical damage, and replace as necessary. Slightly burned contacts should be sanded smooth.

Inspect the spark plug leads and distributor-to-coil high-tension lead for cracks, brittleness, or damaged rubber boots. Replace any deteriorated parts.

While primary wiring is less perishable than the secondary circuit, it should be checked for cracked insulation or loose connections. Tighten connections or replace wires as necessary.

7. Adjust the Ignition Timing.

Timing is adjusted at every tune-up. This is especially important because changing the dwell angle will change the ignition timing. Adjusting the contact points may throw the timing off.

On most vehicles, the engine may be timed with either a test lamp or with a stroboscopic timing light. However, manufacturer's recommendations should be consulted because some engines must be timed under certain operating conditions, while others can only be timed with the engine stopped. On emission-controlled cars, the tune-up sticker will outline the conditions under which the engine is to be timed. These instructions should be followed to the letter and, if a speed is specified, a tachometer should be used to make sure that the speed is correct before timing the engine.

STATIC TIMING

A. Make sure the engine is at the correct temperature for timing adjustment (either fully warmed or cold, as specified in the factory manual or a Chilton's repair manual).

B. Locate no. 1 cylinder and trace its wire back to the distributor cap. Then, remove the cap.

C. Rotate the engine until the proper timing mark on the crankshaft pulley is lined up with the timing mark on the block. Observe the direction of distributor shaft rotation when the engine is turned in its normal direction of rotation.

D. Connect a test lamp from the coil terminal (the distributor side) to ground. Make sure the tip of the rotor lines up with no. 1 cylinder. If it does not, turn the engine one full revolution and line up the timing marks again.

E. Loosen the clamp that holds the distributor in position and turn the distributor body in the direction of normal shaft rotation until the points close and the test lamp goes out. Now turn the distributor in the opposite direction very slowly, just until the test lamp comes on. Tighten the distributor clamp.

F. To test the adjustment, turn the engine backward until the light again goes out, and then forward just until the light comes back on.

NOTE: *Engines with a belt-driven camshaft must not be rotated backward.*

If the timing marks are lined up, the engine is accurately timed. If the timing is too far advanced, loosen the distributor and turn it just slightly in the direction of shaft rotation, and retighten the clamp. If the timing is retarded, turn the distributor in the opposite direction and then repeat the test. Repeat this procedure until the light comes on just as the two timing marks are aligned.

TIMING WITH A STROBOSCOPIC LAMP

A. If the timing light operates from the battery, connect the red lead to the battery positive terminal, and the black lead to a ground. With all lights, connect the trigger lead in series with no. 1 spark plug wire.

B. Disconnect and plug the required vacuum hoses, as in the manufacturer's specifications. Connect the red lead of a tachometer to the distributor side of the coil and the black lead to ground. Start the engine, put the (automatic) transmission in gear (if required), and read the tachometer. Adjust the carburetor idle screw to the proper speed for setting the timing. Aim the timing light at the crankshaft pulley to determine where the timing point is. If the point is hard to see, it may help to stop the engine and mark it with chalk.

C. Loosen the distributor holding clamp and rotate the distributor slowly in either direction until the timing is correct. Tighten the clamp and observe the timing mark again to determine that the timing is still correct. Readjust the position of the distributor, if necessary.

D. Accelerate the engine in Neutral, while watching the timing point. If the distributor advance mechanisms are working, the timing point should advance as the engine is accelerated. If the engine's vacuum advance is engaged with the transmission in Neutral, check the vacuum advance operation by running the engine at about 1,500 rpm and connecting and disconnecting the vacuum advance hose.

8. Adjust the Carburetor.

On most vehicles manufactured before 1972, there are adjustable idle mixture screws. On emission-controlled vehicles, the instructions on the engine compartment sticker or in the manual should be followed explicitly. Generally, the idle mixture is adjusted as follows:

a. Connect a tachometer red lead to the negative terminal of the coil, and ground the black lead. Adjust the carburetor idle screw or solenoid screw to the normal idle speed or to the speed specified for mixture adjustment in the manufacturer's instructions. Solenoid screws should be adjusted with the solenoid disconnected. After adjusting the screw, reconnect the solenoid wire and open the throttle slightly to extend the plunger and check the adjustment.

b. On uncontrolled vehicles, adjust the

mixture screw(s) for the highest idle speed on the tachometer. On emission-controlled vehicles, adjust the screw(s) inward from highest idle until the specified drop in rpm is attained.

c. Reset the carburetor to the specified idle speed.

9. Adjust the Valves.

Periodic valve adjustments are not required on most modern engines with hydraulic valve lifters if the engine has been well maintained and no unusual noises come from the valve train. However, the lifters may be adjusted if excessive wear has occurred in the valve train. Also, on many small engines, solid valve lifters are employed, and must be adjusted at every tune-up.

The valve adjustment is accomplished as follows:

a. Bring the engine to the conditions specified for valve adjustment (cold, hot, or hot and running) by the manufacturer.

b. Remove the valve cover(s). If the valves must be adjusted while the engine is running, oil deflector clips should be installed on each rocker arm to avoid oil spray.

c. If the valves must be adjusted with the engine stopped, follow the manufacturer's instructions for positioning the engine properly. For example, on Volkswagens, no. 1 cylinder is adjusted with no. 1 cylinder on the compression stroke at TDC, no. 2 cylinder with the crankshaft turned 180° backward, etc. If these instructions cannot be located, bring each cylinder to TDC on the compression stroke by turning the engine until both valves are closed and the piston is at TDC, before adjusting its valves.

d. Adjust solid lifters by pushing a leaf type feeler gauge of the specified thickness (consult the manual) between the valve stem and rocker arm. Loosen the locking nut and tighten the screw until a light resistance to the movement of the feeler blade is encountered. Hold the adjusting screw while tightening the locking nut. Some adjusting screws are fitted snugly into the rocker arm so no locknut is required. If the feeler is too snug, the adjustment should be loosened to permit the passage of the blade. Remember that a slightly loose adjustment is easier on the valves than an overly tight one, so adjust the valves accordingly. Always recheck the adjustment after the locknut has been tightened.

Refer to a manual for details on hydraulic valve lifter adjustment.

e. Replace the valve cover, cleaning all traces of old gasket material from both surfaces and installing a new gasket. Tighten valve cover nuts alternately, in several stages, to ensure proper seating.

Emission Control Checks

The PCV valve may be checked for proper function as follows:

1. Start the engine and operate it at normal idle speed.

2. Connect a tachometer between the negative coil terminal (red tach lead) and ground.

3. Note the tach reading, and then pinch off the PCV hose. There should be a

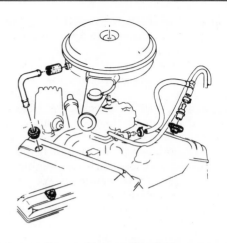

CLOSED POSITIVE
(307, 350 & 400 2-BBL)

A closed PCV system as used on Chevrolet V8 engines (© G.M. Corp)

drop of about 40–80 rpm. Otherwise, the PCV system is clogged, or the valve is faulty. Inspect the hoses for clogging and clean if necessary. If clogging is not found,

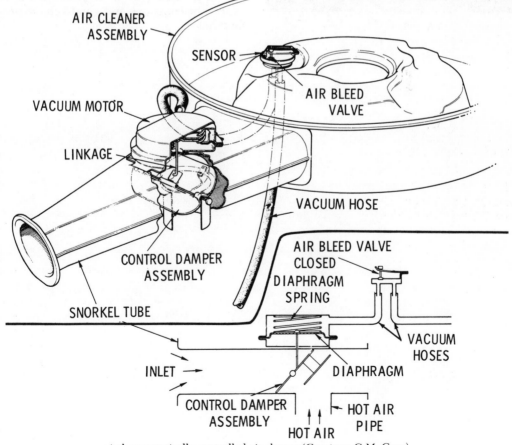

A thermostatically controlled air cleaner (Courtesy, G.M. Corp)

replace the PCV valve. If clogging is found, retest the system, replacing the valve if necessary.

All vacuum hoses should be checked for cracks or loose connections and replaced as necessary. The carburetor air preheating system may be checked by placing a small thermometer inside the air cleaner while the engine is idling. The thermometer should read 85–100° or higher. If the temperature is too low with the engine fully warmed, the thermostatic air preheating system requires repair.

If the vehicle uses an idle stop solenoid

A typical idle stop solenoid (© G.M. Corp)

(see the engine compartment sticker), the idle speed must be checked with the solenoid connected and the plunger extended. Open the throttle to allow the plunger to extend itself. After the normal idle has been checked, disconnect the solenoid. The throttle should close slightly and come to rest at the adjustment of the throttle stop screw or tang. Adjust the screw or bend the tang until the specified slow idle is attained. If the throttle does not close when the solenoid is disconnected, the solenoid or slow idle may be adjusted incorrectly or the throttle linkage may be binding. If adjustments and checking of the linkage reveal no problems, the solenoid will have to be replaced.

Many other types of emission control devices are used to position the throttle under certain operating conditions, or to interrupt and restore vacuum advance, etc. These devices, in many cases, are to be adjusted at each tune-up. It is recommended that a manual be consulted and all tune-up operations and checks required be performed at each tune-up to ensure effective control of emissions and good vehicle performance.

9 · The Electrical System

Basic Electricity

Understanding just a little about the basic theory of electricity will make electrical system troubleshooting much easier. Several gauges are used in electrical troubleshooting to see inside the circuit being tested. Without a basic understanding, it will be difficult to understand testing procedures.

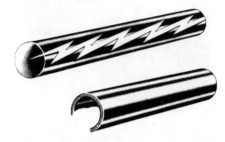

Electricity can be compared to water flowing in a pipe (© G.M. Corp)

Electricity is defined as the flow of electrons. Electrons are hypothetical particles thought to constitute the basic "stuff" of electricity. In a comparison with water flowing in a pipe, the electrons would be the water. As the flow of water can be measured, the flow of electricity can be measured. The unit of measurement is amperes, frequently abbreviated "amps". An ammeter will measure the actual amount of current flowing in the circuit.

Just as water *pressure* is measured in units such as pounds per square inch, electrical pressure is measured in volts. When a voltmeter's two probes are placed on two "live" portions of an electrical circuit with different electrical pressures, current will flow through the voltmeter and produce a reading which indicates the difference in electrical pressure between the two parts of the circuit.

While increasing the voltage in a circuit

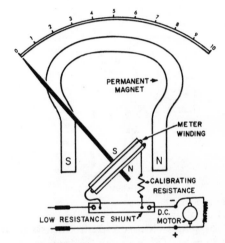

Ammeter circuit

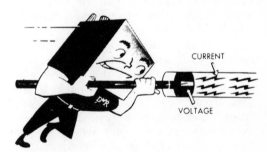

Voltage is the pressure that causes current to flow (© G.M. Corp)

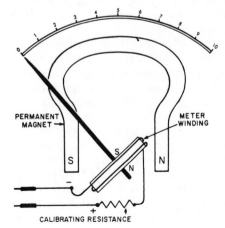

Voltmeter circuit

61

will increase the flow of current, the actual flow depends not only on voltage, but on the resistance of the circuit. The standard unit for measuring circuit resistance is an ohm, measured by an ohmmeter. The ohmmeter is somewhat similar to an ammeter, but incorporates its own source of power so that a standard voltage is always present.

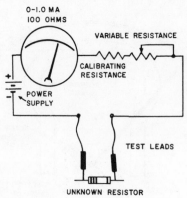

Ohmmeter circuit

An actual electric circuit consists of four basic parts. These are: the power source, such as a generator or battery; a hot wire, which conducts the electricity under a relatively high voltage or pressure to the electrical appliance supplied by the circuit; the load, such as a lamp, motor, resistor, or relay coil; and the ground wire, which carries the current back to the source under very low electrical pressure. In such a circuit, the bulk of the resistance exists between the point where the hot wire is connected to the load, and the point where the load is grounded. In an automobile, the vehicle's frame, which is made of steel, is used as a part of the ground circuit for many of the electrical devices.

Remember that, in electrical testing, the voltmeter is connected in parallel with the circuit being tested (without disconnecting any wires) and measures the difference in voltage between the locations of the two probes; that the ammeter is connected in series with the load (the circuit is separated at one point and the ammeter inserted so it becomes a part of the circuit); and that the ohmmeter is self-powered, so that all the power in the circuit should be off and the portion of the circuit to be measured contacted at either end by one of the probes of the meter.

The Charging System

How It Works

The automobile charging system provides electrical power for operation of the vehicle's ignition and starting systems and all the electrical accessories. The battery serves as an electrical surge or storage tank, storing (in chemical form) the energy originally produced by the engine-driven generator. The system also provides a means of regulating generator output to protect the battery from being overcharged and to avoid excessive voltage to the accessories.

An alternator rotor. Initial current flow comes from the battery (Courtesy of Delco-Remy)

The storage battery is a chemical device incorporating parallel lead plates in a tank containing a sulfuric acid-water solution. Adjacent plates are slightly dissimilar, and the chemical reaction of the two dissimilar plates produces electrical energy when the battery is connected to a load such as the starter motor. The chemical reaction is reversible, so that when the generator is producing a voltage (electrical pressure) greater than that produced by the battery, electricity is forced into the battery, and the battery is returned to its fully charged state.

The vehicle's generator is driven mechanically, through V belts, by the engine crankshaft. It consists of two coils of fine wire, one stationary (the "stator"), and one movable (the "rotor"). The rotor may also be known as the "armature", and consists of fine wire wrapped around an iron core which is mounted on a shaft. The electricity which flows through the two coils of wire (provided initially by the battery in some cases) creates an intense magnetic field around both rotor and stator, and the interaction between the two fields creates voltage, allowing the generator to power the accesories and charge the battery.

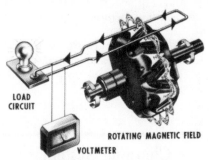

LOAD CIRCUIT

ROTATING MAGNETIC FIELD

VOLTMETER

In an alternator, rotation of the field through the stator windings produces voltage (Courtesy of Delco-Remy)

There are two types of generators; the earlier is the direct current (DC) type. The current produced by the DC generator is generated in the armature and carried off the spinning armature by stationary brushes contacting the commutator. The commutator is a series of smooth metal contact plates on the end of the armature. The commutator plates, which are separated from one another by a very short gap, are connected to the armature circuits so that current will flow in one direction only in the wires carrying the generator output. The generator stator consists of two stationary coils of wire which draw some of the output current of the generator to form a powerful magnetic field and create the interaction of fields which generates the voltage. The generator field is wired in series with the regulator.

Newer automobiles use alternating cur-

A typical alternator (© G.M. Corp)

rent generators or "alternators", because they are more efficient, can be rotated at higher speeds, and have fewer brush problems. In an alternator, the field rotates while all the current produced passes only through the stator windings. The brushes bear against continuous slip rings rather than a commutator. This causes the current produced to periodically reverse the direction of its flow. Diodes (electrical one-way switches) block the flow of curent from traveling in the wrong direction. A series of diodes is wired together to permit the alternating flow of the stator to be converted to a pulsating, but unidirectional flow at the alternator output. The alternator's field is wired in series with the voltage regulator.

The regulator consists of several circuits. Each circuit has a core, or magnetic coil of wire, which operates a switch. Each switch is connected to ground through one or more resistors. The coil of wire responds directly to system voltage. When the voltage reaches the required level, the magnetic field created by the winding of wire closes the switch and inserts a resistance into the generator field circuit, thus reducing the output. The contacts of the switch cycle open and close many times each second to precisely control voltage.

While alternators are self-limiting as far as maximum current is concerned, DC generators employ a current regulating circuit which responds directly to the total amount of current flowing through the generator circuit rather than to the output voltage. The current regulator is similar to the voltage regulator except that all system current must flow through the energizing coil on its way to the various accessories.

SAFETY PRECAUTIONS

Observing these precautions will ensure safe handling of the electrical system components, and will avoid damage to the vehicle's electrical system:

A. Be *absolutely* sure of the polarity of a booster battery before making connections. Connect the cables positive to positive, and negative to negative. Connect positive cables first and then make the last connection to a ground on the body of the booster vehicle so that arcing cannot ignite hydrogen gas that may have accumulated near the battery. Even momentary connection of a booster battery with the polarity reversed will damage alternator diodes.

B. Disconnect both vehicle battery cables before attempting to charge a battery.

C. Never ground the alternator or generator output or battery terminal. Be cautious when using metal tools around a battery to avoid creating a short circuit between the terminals.

D. Never ground the field circuit between the alternator and regulator.

E. Never run an alternator or generator without load unless the field circuit is disconnected.

F. Never attempt to polarize an alternator.

G. Keep the regulator cover in place when taking voltage and current limiter readings.

H. Use insulated tools when adjusting the regulator.

J. Whenever DC generator-to-regulator wires have been disconnected, the generator *must* be repolarized. To do this with an externally grounded, light duty generator, momentarily place a jumper wire between the battery terminal and the generator terminal of the regulator. With an internally grounded heavy duty unit, disconnect the wire to the regulator field terminal and touch the regulator battery terminal with it.

Quick Reference Guide For Charging System Troubleshooting

A. *Inspect the system.* Check the battery electrolyte level, all electrical connections, and the generator (alternator) drive belt condition and tension.

B. *Check the battery.* Test the battery under load. Check the specific gravity of all the battery cells. Charge the battery, if necessary. Replace the battery if it will not respond to charging.

C. *Test the output of the generator (alternator).* Replace or repair if rated output is not produced.

D. *Test charging circuit resistance.* If resistance is too high, replace bad wiring or repair poor connections.

E. *Check voltage and current regulator performance.* If not to specifications, clean contacts, adjust contact gap, and readjust regulator as necessary. Replace a nonadjustable unit which does not regulate the specified voltage. Check the field circuit wiring and replace bad wires or repair poor connections before replacing the regulator.

F. *Troubleshooting chart.* Battery discharge due to electrical system short or ground, generator output drops off at high speeds, etc.

Charging System Troubleshooting

A. Inspect the System.

Check the generator mounts for cracks or loose mounting bolts, and tighten or replace parts as necessary. Check the condition and tension of the drive belt. Replace the belt if it is frayed or cracked. Tighten the belt if there is play or inadequate tension. If manufacturer's specifications and a strand tension gauge are not available, the belt should be tightened so that it can be depressed about $\frac{1}{2}$ in. for each 10 in. of length with moderate (10–15 lbs) thumb pressure.

Check the level of electrolyte in the battery cells and fill them, if necessary, with distilled water to the level of the indicator ring. Clean the surface of the battery with a rag. Replace the battery if there is a sizable crack.

Check the condition of the battery terminals. If there is corrosion, disconnect the terminals and clean them with a baking soda and water solution. Thoroughly clean the corroded material from the conducting surfaces with a wire brush. Reconnect the terminals snugly. Even if no cleaning was required, carefully tighten the terminals. Coat the terminals with clean petroleum jelly to prevent further corrosion.

All the visible wires in the charging system should then be checked for cracked or frayed insulation and loose or corroded connections. Clean any corroded connections with a wire brush or sandpaper, and reconnect them snugly. Replace any frayed wiring.

B. Check the Battery.

Check the capacity of the battery as indicated by a rating on the label in wattage or ampere-hours. Recommended battery rating for the vehicle may be found in the owner's manual. The battery capacity should be at least equal to the recommended rating.

A quick check of battery condition may be made by connecting a voltmeter across the battery posts and cranking the engine for about 15 seconds. If the voltage at the positive terminal remains at approximately 9.6 or above, the battery is most likely in good condition.

If the battery does not pass this test, test the specific gravity of the electrolyte in each of the cells. If the battery requires addition of water to bring the cells to the proper level, this should be done first. If water had to be added, the battery should be charged at a high enough rate to cause gasing (hydrogen emission) of the cells for 15 minutes to ensure thorough mixing of the electrolyte.

Test the specific gravity of each cell with a clean hydrometer. If the hydrometer has a thermometer, draw in and expel the fluid several times to make a thermometer reading. Otherwise use a battery thermometer, allowing time for the thermometer to reach the temperature of the electrolyte. Correct the hydrometer reading by adding 0.004 to it for each 10° over 80° F, and subtracting 0.004 for each 10° below 80° F.

If the readings are more than 50 points apart, the battery should be replaced. The battery is fully charged if gravity is 1.260–1.280, half charged at about 1.210, and fully discharged at about 1.120. If the readings are inconclusive, the battery should be charged at a rate that will not bring the electrolyte to a temperature over 125° F. This should be done until the specific gravity remains constant for two hours. If at this point, all the cells are not between 1.260 and 1.280, especially if the variations exceed 50 points, the battery should be replaced.

There are various commercial battery testers available that measure output voltage while subjecting the battery to a load. They will do an excellent job.

C. Test the Output of the Generator (Alternator).

A quick and simple output test may be made using a voltmeter. Simply connect the voltmeter between the positive and negative battery terminals and measure the voltage. Then start the engine and run it at fast idle. Check the voltage again. If it has risen (usually about 2 V), the generator (alternator) and regulator are functioning.

The regulator may be easily bypassed if a field rheostat is available, in order to see whether an inadequate voltage rise as measured in the above test is due to problems in the generator (alternator) or regulator. Proceed as follows:

1. Disconnect the field wire from the F or FLD terminal on the regulator. Connect the field rheostat between the IGN terminal of the regulator and the disconnected field wire.

2. Turn the rheostat to the maximum resistance position (the low side of the scale).

3. Start the engine and operate it at fast idle. Gradually turn the rheostat control toward the decreased resistance side of the scale while watching the voltmeter. Turn the knob until the voltage read on the meter equals the manufacturer's specified maximum voltage for the generator (alternator). If it will not produce the specified voltage, it requires repair or replacement.

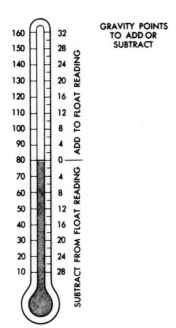

Hydrometer correction chart (Courtesy, Chrysler Corp)

In cases of questionable performance, a more accurate test of generator (alternator) condition is an amperage output test. A DC generator may be tested as described below:

a. Remove the armature and field leads from the generator. Place a jumper wire between these two terminals. Connect a 100 amp capacity ammeter between the generator armature terminal, and whichever battery lead is not grounded, with the positive ammeter lead on the generator.

b. Start the engine, and with the engine idling, move the negative ammeter lead to the positive terminal of the battery.

c. Run the engine at fast idle and note the generator output as measured on the ammeter. Compare with manufacturer's specifications. Output should be about 30 amps for regular-duty equipment, and about 50 amps for heavy-duty units.

NOTE: *Disconnect all leads as soon as the engine stops or else battery current will flow through the generator.*

Alternator output tests very according to the design of the alternator and regulator in use. For the details of testing an alternator-powered charging system, it is recommended that a Chilton manual or factory repair manual be consulted. The alternator output test is generally accomplished as follows:

a. Place an ammeter in series between the battery terminal of the alternator and the disconnected battery lead.

b. Hook up a voltmeter between the battery lead on the alternator and the battery negative terminal. Ground or connect the alternator field terminal to the battery positive post. (This will depend on the internal design of the regulator.)

c. Hook a carbon pile rheostat between the two battery posts. Connect a tachometer to the engine.

d. Start the engine and adjust to the speed specified in the test instructions. Adjust the carbon pile rheostat so the voltage at which the test is to be performed registers on the voltmeter, then read the amperage on the ammeter.

e. If amperage is below specifications, the alternator requires repairs. Some test instructions include procedures for evaluating the alternator condition and locating the problem based on the difference between rated amperage and what is found in the test.

D. Test the Charging Circuit Resistance

The charging circuit resistance test is very similar to the output test for both generators and alternators. A manual should be consulted for details of instrument hook-up and amperage settings, as well as the maximum permissible voltage drop (usually less than 1 V).

The test differs in that the voltmeter is connected between the generator battery terminal and the positive terminal of the vehicle's battery. The engine is operated at fast idle, and the carbon pile rheostat adjusted until a specified amperage is flowing to the battery. The voltage drop is then compared to specifications. If voltage drop is excessive, the connections must be carefully inspected and, if necessary, cleaned and tightened. If this fails to bring the voltage drop down to specifications, wiring must be replaced.

E. Check Voltage and Current Regulator Performance.

A very simple test of regulator performance may be made as follows:

1. Remove the high-tension lead from the coil and ground it. Crank the engine for about 30 seconds.

2. Disconnect the battery terminal of the regulator, or the alternator-to-battery cable on alternators with integral regulators, and insert an ammeter. The ammeter leads will have to be reversed (with the engine off) if the ammeter reads downscale.

3. Reconnect the distributor high-tension lead and start the engine, running it at fast idle. Watch the ammeter. The amperage reading should be high at first, and then, after two or three minutes of operation, it should fall off to a very low reading, assuming that all vehicle accessories are turned off.

If this test reveals problems, the regulator should be further tested. General test instructions follow. Manufacturer's specifications should be consulted for the exact voltage output required at various regulator temperatures.

Voltage Regulator Test

This test requires a voltmeter and ammeter. For Delco units, a 0.25 ohm resistor of 25 watt capacity is required. In the case of the Chrysler mechanical regulator with alternator, a carbon pile rheostat is required.

A. Hook up the test equipment as described below. Delco DC Generator: Connect the resistor in series between the battery and regulator by removing the line to the regulator "Batt" terminal and inserting the resistor between the terminal and the wire connection. Connect a voltmeter between the regulator terminal and a good ground.

Autolite or Ford DC Generator: Connect an ammeter between the battery and the regulator by disconnecting the line to the "Batt" terminal and inserting the ammeter. Connect the voltmeter between the armature connection on the regulator and ground.

Chrysler Mechanical Regulator with Alternator: Connect the voltmeter between the ignition terminal no. 1 of the ballast resistor and ground. Connect a carbon pile rheostat between the two battery terminals, with the resistance adjusted to the highest level.

Chrysler Electronic Regulator: Disconnect the battery during hook-up. Connect the ammeter between the alternator and battery by disconnecting the battery-to-alternator lead and inserting the ammeter (with the positive side toward the alternator). Connect the voltmeter between the "Ign" terminal of the regulator and a good ground.

Delco 5.5 and 6.2 alternators: Connect the resistor between the battery cable (with the cable disconnected) and the battery cable connection on the junction block. Connect the voltmeter between that junction block connection and a ground on the body of the relay.

B. Start the engine and run it at fast idle (about 1,600 rpm) for 15 minutes to bring all components to operating temperature. If you are testing a Chrysler alternator with a mechanical regulator, adjust the engine speed to 1,250 rpm with a tachometer, and adjust the carbon pile rheostat so the charging rate is 15 amps. With Delcotron alternators, turn on the headlights and heater blower. With Ford DC units, turn on accessories until the generator is producing 8–10 amps. With Autolite DC units, turn accessories until one half of the generator output is being produced.

C. Place a thermometer on the regulator to measure its temperature. Stop and start

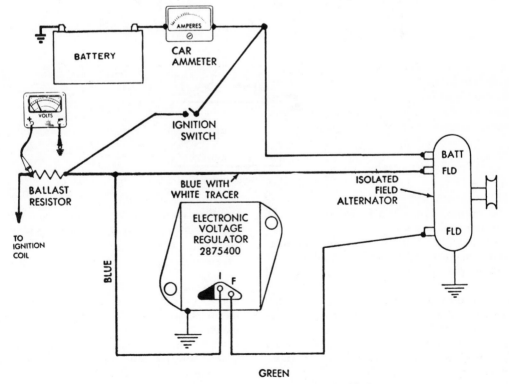

Voltage regulator test hookup—Chrysler isolated field alternator

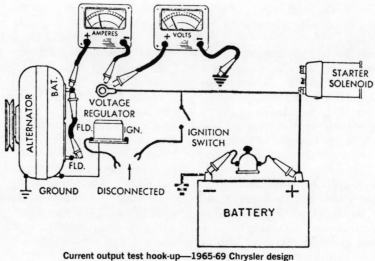

Current output test hook-up—1965-69 Chrysler design

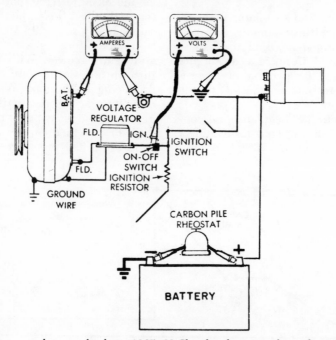

Voltage regulator test hookup—1965–69 Chrysler electro-mechanical regulator

the engine after 15 minutes to cycle the regulator off and on.

D. Read the voltage and temperature, and compare each with manufacturer's specifications. On Chrysler mechanical units with an alternator, the lower contacts must also be tested by bringing the engine speed to 2,200 rpm and adjusting the carbon pile for 7 amps charging rate.

If the results of this test do not meet specifications, or if the battery is overcharged (loses water continuously), or if starting problems are encountered with no problems in the battery or starting system, the regulator should be adjusted and serviced or, if necessary, replaced.

REGULATOR ADJUSTMENT

1968–72 Ford and 1970–72 Chrysler regulators are not adjustable. If these units do not meet specifications, they must be replaced.

All mechanical units may be adjusted by either turning an adjusting screw or bending a spring mount to increase the tension of a spring to increase the voltage

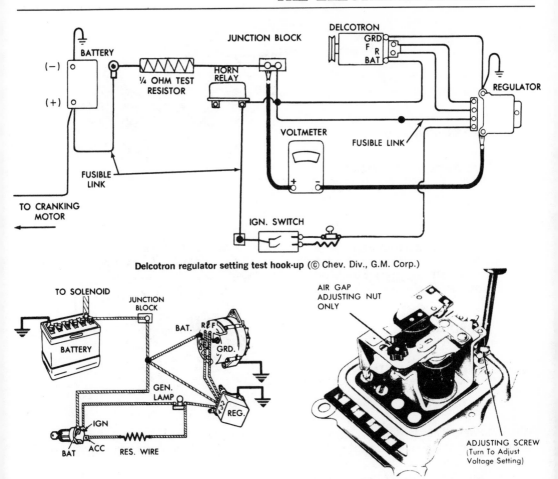

Delcotron regulator setting test hook-up (© Chev. Div., G.M. Corp.)

Part A. Delcotron regulator setting test hookup (Courtesy Chevrolet Div. of General Motors Corp); *Part B.* Typical Delcotron circuit diagram (Courtesy Chevrolet Div. of General Motors Corp); *Part C.* Adjusting voltage setting—mechanical regulator (Courtesy Chevrolet Div. of General Motors Corp)

and decreasing the tension of the spring to lower the output voltage. General Motors solid-state regulators which are separate from the alternator may be adjusted by removing a pipe plug in the top of the regulator and turning the adjusting screw underneath.

Specific manufacturer's instructions and specifications for each type of regulator should be consulted. All final regulator checks must be accomplished with the regulator cover in place.

If the regulator contact points are burned or pitted, they should be cleaned with a riffler file and the gap should be adjusted according to the manufacturer's

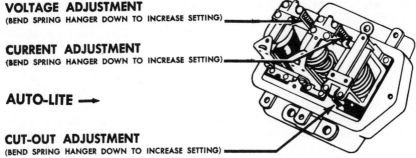

Adjusting an Autolite D.C. voltage regulator

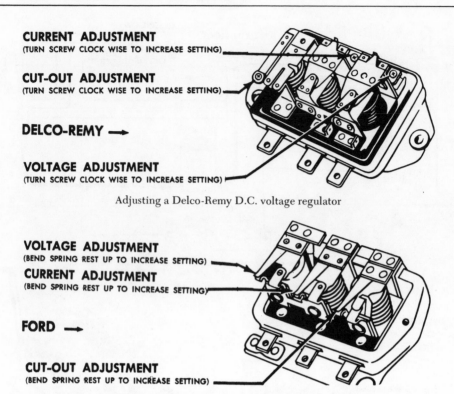

CURRENT ADJUSTMENT
(TURN SCREW CLOCK WISE TO INCREASE SETTING)

CUT-OUT ADJUSTMENT
(TURN SCREW CLOCK WISE TO INCREASE SETTING)

DELCO-REMY →

VOLTAGE ADJUSTMENT
(TURN SCREW CLOCK WISE TO INCREASE SETTING)

Adjusting a Delco-Remy D.C. voltage regulator

VOLTAGE ADJUSTMENT
(BEND SPRING REST UP TO INCREASE SETTING)
CURRENT ADJUSTMENT
(BEND SPRING REST UP TO INCREASE SETTING)

FORD →

CUT-OUT ADJUSTMENT
(BEND SPRING REST UP TO INCREASE SETTING)

Adjusting a Ford D.C. voltage regulator

specifications. This is done by closing the contacts and then measuring the distance between the armature and core of the regulator with a round feeler gauge. Bend the contact arm at the specified spot until the gap is correct.

In the case of DC regulators which fail to produce adequate output only under heavy load conditions, the current regulator may be checked. An ammeter is placed in series with the battery, and the amperage is read just after a very heavy load has been placed on the battery by cranking the engine for 30 seconds with the high-tension lead to the coil grounded. All accessories should be turned on for the test. The current should meet manufacturer's specifications. The current regulator is adjusted in the same way as the voltage regulator.

If the regulator produces insufficient voltage or does not regulate the voltage properly, and cannot be adjusted, it should be replaced. If voltage output is inadequate, the connections in the field circuit between the regulator and generator (alternator) should be cleaned and tightened, and the wires should be checked for continuity. Rectify any problems found by re-placing wires or cleaning and tightening connections before condemning the regulator.

Dash Gauges and Indicators

Dash gauges and indicators permit the driver to monitor the operating conditions of his engine and charging system, and the level of fuel in his fuel tank. Generally, the engine gauges monitor the oil pressure and the coolant temperature. Engine warning lights come on if oil pressure drops to a level that cannot ensure adequate protection of the engine's moving parts from heat and wear, or if coolant temperature rises to the point where coolant will be lost through boiling. Oil and coolant gauges are usually marked to indicate safe operating ranges.

The ammeter tells the driver whether current is flowing to or from the battery, and reports the amount. Charging system warning lights tell the driver whether or not the generator is operating. They do not give an indication of charging rate.

The fuel gauge reports the level of fuel

Charging System Troubleshooting Chart

Indication:	*Cause:*
Generator output is good at low rpm, but suddenly drops off as speed is increased.	Loose wire in rotor slung out by centrifugal force, shorting to stator windings.
Constant slight battery drain; starting voltage is low, but only after overnight shutdown.	Ground in wiring harness or an accessory. (Disconnect battery positive cable, insert a voltmeter, and check for voltage. If there is a reading, a very small ground exists in the wiring harness.)
Battery discharges within a few hours of shutdown; a constant sizable drain.	Battery may have an internal ground: in this case, the system will show symptoms of overcharging, even though your voltage regulator is all right. Alternator may have a shorted positive diode, closing field relay and permitting constant discharge through the alternator.
Indicator light is off at all times, preventing alternator operation.	Faulty bulb, socket, or wiring. Also, regulator wiring may be at fault.
Indicator light on at all times.	Improper field relay or generator cutout adjustment, or faulty unit.
Battery slightly discharged.	Voltage limiter setting low, or generator (alternator) rating not sufficient for the accessory load. Added accessories may be the cause.
Battery overcharged.	Voltage regulator set too high for the operating conditions. Faulty resistor or coil in regulator, or poor ground between regulator and alternator.
Noisy alternator.	Loose mountings. Slipping belt. Bad bearings. Faulty rectifier (if the noise sounds electrical).
Ammeter fluctuates or headlights flicker.	Bad generator brushes, improperly set regulator, or poor connections in charging system, or faulty regulator.
Regulator points burn or stick.	Poor ground between generator and regulator, or burned regulator resistor.

in the tank, as measured by a tank float. Most such gauges are marked to indicate the level in increments of quarters of a tank.

While gauges indicate operating conditions over a wide range, warning lights are more easily noticed when trouble occurs suddenly.

Most gauge problems result from faulty wiring or connections, a faulty sensor, or a faulty gauge. In some cases a problem in several gauges at once is due to a malfunction in a special voltage regulator that supplies all the gauges. Because gauge parts are fairly inexpensive, troubleshooting in this area usually involves identifying the defective sensor, wiring, gauge, or gauge voltage regulator, and replacing the faulty unit. It should also be remembered that when many gauges malfunction at once, or repeated gauge problems occur, the voltage regulator in the charging system may be at fault.

GAUGE OPERATION

Bourdon Tube Gauges

This type of gauge is used to measure oil pressure or engine temperature. It responds to changes in pressure via a Bourdon tube which is a coil of tubing with a flattened side. As pressure rises inside the tubing, the flattened side tends to bow somewhat and straighten the coil. The

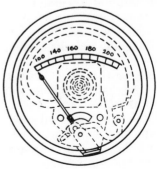

A bourdon tube type temperature gauge

gauge needle is linked directly to the end of the tube.

When used as an oil pressure gauge, the unit responds directly to the pressure generated by the oil pump, although the gauge and the line to the oil system are kept full of air to make sure that pulsations from the oil pump are dampened out. If the gauge reads accurately but pulsates, the problem may be cured by draining the oil line and gauge and reconnecting all fittings more snugly. If there is evidence of leaks, replace the faulty parts. Reconnect the line at the gauge first, and then at the engine.

If the gauge fails to respond properly, remove the line at the gauge and place it over an empty container. Then start the engine. If oil does not flow from the line after expulsion of a few bubbles, blow out the line to allow pressure to reach the gauge.

If the gauge is still in question, the best procedure is to connect a gauge of known accuracy into the system to determine that engine oil pressure is adequate and that the gauge line is clear. Replace the gauge if the good unit operates properly.

When this type of gauge is used to measure engine temperature, it responds to pressure generated by a volatile liquid sealed in a sensing bulb. The bulb is placed in or near the engine cooling water. The vapor pressure of the fluid varies directly with the temperature and the Bourdon tube and gauge are calibrated to reflect the temperature on the face of the gauge. This type of unit is entirely sealed. If the gauge simply does not move from the minimum reading, it may be assumed that the gauge, line, or sensing bulb has leaked, and the whole unit must be replaced. If readings are questionable, a unit of known accuracy may be substituted. If that unit performs accurately, the faulty unit should be replaced.

If the unit responds, but reads slightly low at all times, test the cooling system thermostat to make sure that it is operating properly. If that unit tests out, but the gauge reading has fallen substantially, the gauge unit is faulty.

Install the new unit carefully. Form a loop in the line somewhere between the engine and the gauge to minimize the effect of vibration on the gauge and sensing bulb.

Bimetal Gauges

These gauges employ a bimetallic strip to sense current flow. The two metals which make up this strip expand at different rates. As the temperature of the strip changes, therefore, the two metals work against each other, making the strip bend back and forth. The free end of the strip operates the gauge needle through a simple linkage.

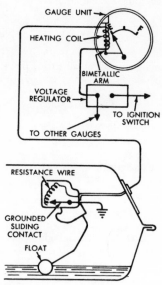

Fuel gauge circuit

In the case of a fuel tank bimetal gauge, the sensing unit consists of a resistor and sliding contact. The position of the contact is determined by a float. As the sliding contact moves across the resistor, current is sent in varying amounts to the gauge or to ground. The current which flows to the gauge passes through a resistor which surrounds the bimetal strip, so the gauge indication varies with the position of the float in the tank.

When a bimetal gauge is used to sense engine temperature, the resistor and sliding contact are replaced by a resistor which changes its resistance with temperature. The resistor unit is immersed in the cooling water or placed in direct contact with the material of the engine block.

A bimetal gauge may also be used to measure oil pressure. In this application, the sending unit's linkage to the sliding contact is activated by a diaphragm, one side of which is exposed to engine oil pressure.

The bimetal gauge may be tested by removing it from the dash and applying voltage to it with flashlight batteries. If the gauge is the type that uses a constant voltage regulator, it operates at three volts (3 V). If other gauges are also malfunctioning, the constant voltage regulator is at fault.

To test a constant voltage type gauge, apply 3 V, using two flashlight cells in series and jumper wires. If the gauge operates at line voltage, use four batteries in series to provide 6 V. Under these conditions, the 3 V gauge will read full scale, while the 12 V unit will read half-scale. Replace the unit if it fails to read properly.

If the gauge checks out, or if replacing a faulty unit fails to correct the problem, the sending unit should be tested. Fuel gauge sending units should be removed from the tank and tested for continuity (with an ammeter) through the full range of float movement. If the unit shows zero resistance at any or all positions, it should be replaced. The float should also be checked for leaks. Check the mechanism for binding. Repair or replace the unit as necessary.

The only way to test oil pressure and temperature gauge sending units used with bimetal gauges is to substitute a good unit in place of the suspected one and operate the engine to check for normal response.

If the sending unit proves faulty, it must be replaced. If the problem does not lie in the sending unit, the wire between the sending unit and the gauge should be checked for continuity with an ohmmeter. Check also for bad connections. Clean and tighten connections or replace wiring as necessary.

Magnetic Gauges

The magnetic gauge employs two electromagnetic coils of different sizes to influence the position of the gauge pointer. The smaller coil, located on the left side of the gauge and known as the battery coil, pulls the needle toward the downscale side at all times. This coil receives a constant supply of current directly from the ignition switch. The larger coil, known as the ground coil, receives all of the current passing through the unit to ground when full scale readings are required. Under all other circumstances, varying amounts of the current are passed through the sending unit to ground. When less than full current passes through the ground coil, the battery

coil pulls the pointer over toward the low side of the scale. The sending units for fuel and temperature gauges of this type work on the same principles that apply to the sending units used with bimetal fuel and temperature gauges. The two types of sending units resemble one another closely. However, units designed for one type of gauge cannot be used with the other. It is, therefore, necessary to use only the proper sending unit for the particular gauge.

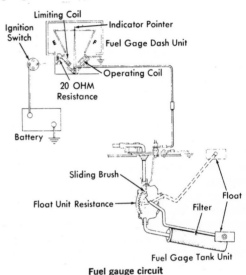

Fuel gauge circuit

Fuel gauge circuit

TESTING GAUGES

Magnetic Fuel Gauges

To test the dash gauge, use a tank unit of known accuracy. Pull the wire from the tank unit and install it on the unit being used for the test. Ground the body of the unit being used for the test. Moving the float arm through its entire range should produce a consistent response from the gauge, with the needle moving from empty to full positions.

If the gauge reads properly, the problem is in the tank unit. Remove it and check for a gas-logged float, binding float, or lack of continuity somewhere in the operating range of the float arm. Replace or repair parts of the unit as necessary.

If the problem does not lie in the sending unit, check all the connections between the sending unit and the dash gauge. Also, check the wire between the dash gauge and the tank unit for continu-

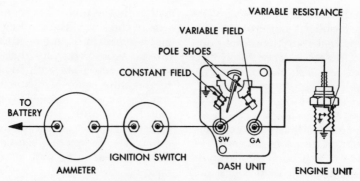

Water temperature gauge

ity. If wiring and connections are all right, or if rectifying problems in them does not give accurate readings, replace the dash gauge.

Magnetic Temperature Gauges

First, disconnect the wire at the sending unit. The gauge hand should be in the cold position. Ground the wire which goes to the sending unit. The gauge should move to the hot position.

If the gauge does not read cold when the wire to the sending unit is disconnected, either the gauge is defective or the wire is grounded somewhere. Disconnect the wire that goes to the sending unit at the gauge. If the gauge now reads cold, replace the wire. Otherwise, replace the gauge unit.

If the gauge reads to the cold side when the wire is disconnected, but does not move to the hot side when it is grounded, ground the sending unit terminal of the gauge. If this causes the gauge to read to the hot side, replace the wire that goes to the sending unit.

If there is no response from the gauge when the sending unit terminal is grounded, test for voltage with a voltmeter or test lamp at the ignition switch terminal of the gauge. If there is no voltage here, test for voltage at the ignition switch accessory terminal. If there is voltage at the ignition switch terminal, replace the wire between this terminal and the gauge. Otherwise, replace the ignition switch.

If this does not produce accurate readings, remove the engine thermostat and test it for proper operation as described in the cooling system troubleshooting section. If the thermostat is all right, or if replacing it does not rectify the problem, substitute a good sending unit for the one pres-

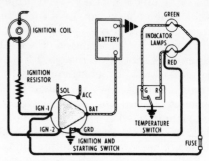

Temperature indicator circuit

ently in the engine block. If this does not produce good readings, replace the dash gauge.

WARNING LIGHTS

Warning lights continuously receive voltage whenever the ignition switch is turned on. The circuit is completed to ground whenever the sending unit contacts close, allowing current to flow through the light.

Oil pressure warning light sending units consist of a diaphragm which responds to about five lbs oil pressure, opening the contacts when that pressure level is exceeded. Water temperature warning lights are energized when a bimetal element closes the contacts in the sending unit at a predetermined water temperature.

TESTING WARNING LIGHTS

Oil Pressure Warning Lights

If the oil light is on all the time, remove the connection at the sending unit. If the light is still on, the problem is a ground between the light and sending unit. Replace the wire between these two units.

If the light goes off when the wire is removed, connect a pressure gauge into the fitting where the oil pressure sending unit is normally installed. If the oil pressure exceeds five lbs, replace the sending unit. Otherwise, there is a mechanical problem causing low oil pressure.

If the light never operates, remove the wire from the sending unit and ground it. If this causes the light to come on, replace the sending unit. If there is no response, check for voltage at both terminals of the lamp socket and at the ignition switch accessory terminal. The faulty unit lies between a hot and a dead terminal. If the lamp socket is suspected, replace the lamp with one that is known to operate. If this produces no response, replace the socket.

Temperature Warning Lights

See the cooling system service section for procedures on testing this system. If the light does not operate in spite of coolant loss, the antifreeze strength, radiator cap, and cooling system pressure tests should be performed. If the light operates even though no coolant is lost, check the radiator cap and thermostat, and, if necessary, clean the system.

If these system tests do not uncover the problem, the light should be tested as outlined for the oil pressure light test above. If the system is known to operate properly, but the light comes on when it should not, or does not come on when overheating occurs, the sending unit should be replaced.

Fuses, Circuit Breakers, and Fusible Links

Fuses are replaceable electrical conductors sealed in small glass cylinders for protection against dust and corrosion. The conducting portion of the fuse is made of a metal with a low melting point. The fuse is designed so that if the amperage passing through it exceeds its rated capacity, the conducting material will melt and interrupt the flow of current through the circuit.

Circuit breakers are electrical switches that employ bimetallic elements to open the circuit whenever current exceeds a specified level. The heat from the passage of current through the unit bends the bimetallic arm to open the contacts of the

switch. After a short period of cooling, the contacts close again.

Circuit breakers are usually used to protect heavy-duty electric motors that can be operated only intermittently. These motors power such auxiliaries as power windows, convertible tops, and tailgates.

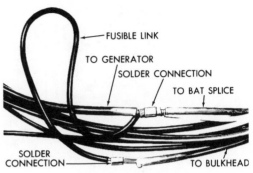

A typical fusible link (© G.M. Corp)

Fusible links are sections of vehicle wiring designed to protect the wiring itself, as well as individual accessories. The links consist of wiring sections about four gauges smaller (larger numerically) than the regular wiring. If a severe overload occurs, the link will burn out entirely before the regular vehicle wiring is damaged.

Repair a burned out fusible link as follows:

A. Disconnect the battery. Cut out all remaining portions of the burned out link. Strip the main wiring insulation back about ½ in. on either end.

B. Solder in a 10 in. long link of wire that is four gauges smaller than the wire to be protected. Use resin core solder only.

C. Tape all exposed portions of the wire securely. Reconnect the battery.

Windshield Wiper Systems

Most windshield wipers are powered by small electric motors of either the permanent magnet or electromagnet type. Some systems are powered by hydraulic pressure from the power steering pump or by intake manifold vacuum.

The wiper systems usually provide two or three operating speeds. Speed is controlled by inserting a resistor into the circuit in the lower speed or speeds. The resistance element may either be located on

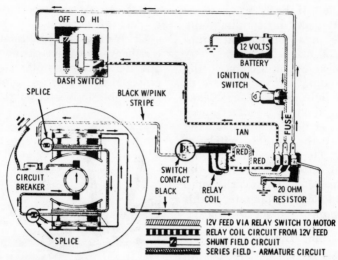

OFF LO HI

DASH SWITCH

SPLICE

BLACK W/PINK STRIPE

12 VOLTS
BATTERY

IGNITION SWITCH

FUSE

TAN

RED

RED

CIRCUIT BREAKER

SWITCH CONTACT

BLACK

RELAY COIL

20 OHM RESISTOR

SPLICE

12V FEED VIA RELAY SWITCH TO MOTOR
RELAY COIL CIRCUIT FROM 12V FEED
SHUNT FIELD CIRCUIT
SERIES FIELD - ARMATURE CIRCUIT

General Motors round motor low-speed circuit (Courtesy G.M. Corp)

the wiper switch or on the wiper motor itself. Most electrical systems employ a circuit breaker which may be located on either the switch or the motor.

If the system does not operate at all, make sure that the blades are not frozen in place or adjusted so the motor cannot reach a park position. Pull the blades outward, then turn on the ignition and wiper switches and check the response. If the blades now move, adjust the blades so that when the motor is parked, they just reach the bottom of the windshield.

If the system does not operate at all, or does not park properly, an electrical check should be made to see if the problem is in the wiring, switch, or motor. If the motor operates but there is no response from the wipers, the gearbox on the motor is at fault.

Locate the wiper switch and test the terminal for the wire from the ignition switch for voltage. If there is no voltage, check for voltage at each connection between the wiper switch and the ignition switch and replace fuses or wiring as necessary.

If there is voltage to the switch but the system does not operate, remove the switch from the dash. Locate a factory manual for the vehicle. Perform a continuity test with an ohmmeter according to the instructions in the manual. This will involve testing for continuity between various terminals with the wiper switch in different positions. Replace the switch if continuity does not exist in one of the tests.

If the switch is good and the wipers still do not perform properly, check the wiring between the switch and the wiper motor. Each wire should be checked for continuity. If all wires are good, or if replacing any defective wire does not rectify the problem, the problem is a mechanical or electrical malfunction in the wiper motor.

Lighting, Turn Signals, and Warning Flashers

The first step in checking any lighting problem is to inspect all wiring and connectors. Make sure all insulation is sound and that all connectors in the circuits involved are securely connected. Also, make sure that the battery and charging systems are in good condition.

TROUBLESHOOTING

Headlamps

If a headlamp does not operate on one or both dimmer positions, substitute a lamp that is known to be good (perhaps the one from the other side of the car), or check for voltage at all terminals of the connector. All should have voltage in at least one of the dimmer positions. If all have voltage, replace the lamp.

If the connector at the lamp does not check out, check for voltage at the dimmer switch. Regardless of the type of switch, voltage should exist at all the terminals in at least one of the switch positions. If the dimmer switch is all right, replace wiring or correct loose connections between the switch and the headlight connector. If there is voltage anywhere in the switch, but one or more of the terminals has no voltage in either switch position, replace the switch.

If there is no voltage to the switch, check for voltage at each connection back to the battery. The faulty component is between a hot connection and a dead one. Replace wiring, fuses, or the headlight switch as necessary.

Direction Signals and Warning Flashers

If one of the direction signal lamps fails to operate, turn on the four-way flasher and check all lamps for operation. If the lamps operate with the flasher on, the defect is in the direction signal flasher or connections.

If the same lamp(s) fails to operate, substitute a lamp that is known to be good for the faulty lamp in each case. If this fails to correct the problem, check for voltage at each connection right back to the flasher. Also check for a corroded socket which might prevent proper grounding of the lamp, and clean up the socket as necessary. The faulty connector or wire is between a hot connection and a dead one. Replace wiring as necessary.

If all the lamps operate, and the direction signal or four-way flasher does not flash, replace the flasher unit. Remember that the unit flashes on and off by means of a bimetal strip that is heated by current flow. If any lamp is not getting current, the flasher will not operate properly.

If it is suspected that the flasher is faulty, it may be tested in either of two ways. If a replacement flasher is available, the wires may be removed from the one installed in the car and connected to the replacement flasher without removing the original unit. If this flasher works properly, replace the original one.

The flasher may also be tested for continuity by consulting a factory service manual for a table that lists which terminals should have continuity in the various switch positions.

If the flasher is not at fault, the wiring between the flasher and the battery or ignition switch should be tested for continuity. Replace wiring, fuses, or connectors as necessary.

10 · The Air Conditioning System

How It Works

The automotive air conditioning system's basic purpose is to reverse the normal flow of heat. Heat normally flows from an area at a certain temperature to any cooler area. The car's air conditioning system must keep the passenger compartment below the outside temperature by continuously removing heat.

This is accomplished by a mechanical compressor which is driven off the engine's crankshaft to compress a material which can be readily changed from a liquid to a gas state. The refrigerant in automotive applications is R-12 which has a $-27°$ F boiling point at atmospheric pressure.

The R-12 is metered into a cooling coil (very similar in construction to a car radiator) at about 30 psi. The refrigerant is in liquid form at this point in the cycle. Its boiling point at 30 psi is just above the

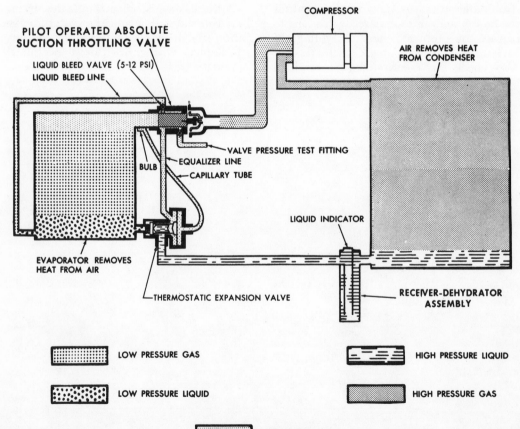

COMPRESSOR

PILOT OPERATED ABSOLUTE
SUCTION THROTTLING VALVE

AIR REMOVES HEAT
FROM CONDENSER

LIQUID BLEED VALVE (5-12 PSI)
LIQUID BLEED LINE

VALVE PRESSURE TEST FITTING

BULB — EQUALIZER LINE

— CAPILLARY TUBE

LIQUID INDICATOR

EVAPORATOR REMOVES
HEAT FROM AIR

THERMOSTATIC EXPANSION VALVE

RECEIVER-DEHYDRATOR
ASSEMBLY

LOW PRESSURE GAS

HIGH PRESSURE LIQUID

LOW PRESSURE LIQUID

HIGH PRESSURE GAS

SUPERHEATED GAS

The refrigeration cycle (© G.M. Corp)

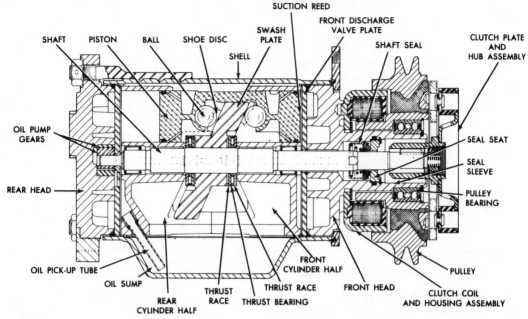

A General Motors type compressor (© G.M. Corp)

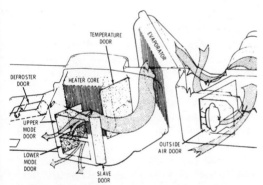

Air flow through the evaporator (Courtesy, G.M. Corp)

normal freezing temperature of water. The refrigerant therefore tends to boil, absorbing heat from the coil.

The cooling coil is known as the evaporator. It is normally located inside the car or on the firewall. A blower forces either outside or inside air, depending on the type of system and the control settings, through the evaporator. The air then passes into the passenger compartment through dash-mounted registers. As the air passes through the evaporator coil, heat and moisture are removed.

The refrigerant boils completely inside the evaporator and then passes into the compressor where its pressure is vastly increased. The pressure on the refrigerant as it leaves the compressor is usually 200 psi or more.

The refrigerant then enters the condenser, a heat exchanging coil usually located in front of the car's radiator. The very high pressure generated in the compressor is put to work at this point and raises the boiling point of the R-12 to over 150° F. When the cooling effect of the outside air is transmitted to the refrigerant through the thin tubes and fins of the condenser coil, it cools and changes back to a liquid, losing the heat it picked up from the interior of the car in the boiling process.

The liquified refrigerant then enters the receiver-drier, a small black tank located next to the condenser or on one of the fender wells. This unit has the job of separating liquid refrigerant from any gas that might have left the condenser, and also filters the refrigerant and absorbs any moisture it may contain. It incorporates a sight glass, in most systems, that allows the refrigerant returning to the evaporator to be checked for the presence of gas bubbles.

The refrigerant then flows through a liquid line to the expansion valve. This valve is located near the evaporator, usually (on most factory systems) on or near the firewall. On aftermarket systems, it is located under the dash. It is shaped like a mushroom, and in some systems incorporates the sight glass. This is the valve which controls the flow of refrigerant to the evaporator. The flow is controlled to supply only that amount the evaporator can handle.

The compressor incorporates a magnetic clutch to permit it to be turned off when it is not required. The clutch is operating whenever the flat portion on the front is turning with the belt-driven pulley located on the front of the compressor.

WARNING: *Because of the dangerous pressures and temperatures associated with the escape of refrigerant, repairs involving a line or fitting that contains refrigerant should always be left to trained servicemen.*

Air Conditioning System Troubleshooting

A. Check the Compressor Belts.

Inspect the compressor belts for cracks or glazing. Cracks that will affect operation of the belt appear as a separation of a large portion of the lower section of the belt. Glazing is the result of slippage, and is indicated by an absolutely smooth appearance of the two belt surfaces that bear against the pulley grooves.

If the belt is cracked or glazed, replace it. Use only the belt specified for the application. Replace multiple belts with new, matched sets, even if one of the belts is still serviceable.

When replacing the belt:

1. Loosen the mounting bolts of the compressor and move the unit toward the fan so that the new belt can be installed without prying.

2. Tighten the belt by pulling the compressor away from the fan, prying it carefully with a breaker bar or, if the mount is provided with a square hole, by applying torque on the mount with the square end of a socket drive. Position the compressor and then tighten all the mounting bolts.

Belts should be tightened so that there is no slack and so they have a springy feel. Applying moderate thumb pressure should cause the belt to yield about ½–¾ in. for each 10 in. between the two pulleys. New belts should be slightly tighter to allow for tension loss during break-in.

Tighten all belts to these specifications,

even if there is no evidence of wear. If the belt is noisy, the problem is usually slippage which can be cured by proper adjustment or replacement.

B. Make Sure the Compressor Is Turning.

The front portion of the clutch remains stationary when the clutch is disengaged, even when the car's engine is operating. If that portion of the clutch turns with the pulley and belts, the compressor is operating.

If the compressor is not running, make sure that the air conditioning is turned on and that the controls are set for full cold. Also, the compressor of many units will not run if outside temperature is below 50° F. If all the switches are set properly and the weather is warm, the compressor should run at least intermittently. If there is no response, pull the wire from the connection on the clutch and test for voltage with a voltmeter. If voltage exists, the clutch is faulty and will have to be replaced. If there is no voltage, trace the wiring back toward the ignition switch. If the wire leads to a device mounted onto the receiver drier, or mounted on the firewall and electrically connected to the back of the compressor, the system has a low refrigerant protection system. If voltage exists on the ignition switch side of this unit but not on the clutch side, the system's refrigerant has leaked out. In this instance, repair by a professional air conditioning mechanic is required.

Otherwise, check each connection for voltage all the way back to the ignition switch. Lack of current can be caused by faulty wiring, bad connections, a blown fuse, or an inoperative thermostat (located right behind the temperature control). Fuses may be checked by removing them and checking for continuity with an ohmmeter. The faulty component lies between the last dead connection and the first to show voltage. Repair wiring, fuses, or switches as necessary.

C. Inspect the Condenser and Fan.

Inspect the condenser for bent fins or foreign material. Straighten the fins and clean them, if necessary.

NOTE: *Be careful, when straightening fins, not to allow the tools being used to damage the condenser tubing.*

Check the fan for bent blades or improper operation caused by slipping belts or a faulty fan clutch. See the cooling system troubleshooting section. Any cooling system problem can contribute to inferior air conditioner performance.

D. Check for Leaks.

Refrigerant system leaks show up as oily areas on the various components because the compressor oil is transported around the entire system along with the refrigerant. Look for oily spots on all the hoses and lines and at the hose and tubing connections, especially. If there are oily deposits, the system may have a leak and should be checked as in subsection E. A small area of oil on the front of the compressor is normal.

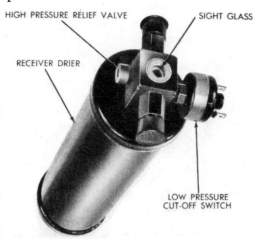

HIGH PRESSURE RELIEF VALVE   SIGHT GLASS

RECEIVER DRIER

LOW PRESSURE CUT-OFF SWITCH

A receiver-drier showing location of the sight glass (Courtesy, Chrysler Corporation)

E. Check the Appearance of the Sightglass.

Start the engine and put the idle speed screw on one of the lower steps of the fast idle cam. Set the blower for high speed and set the thermostat for the lowest possible setting. Locate the sightglass, remove any protective covers, and clean it with a rag. Have someone turn on the air conditioner while you watch the sightglass. The glass should foam and then become clear. After a few minutes of operation, the glass should be entirely clear unless outside temperature is below 70° F. A few bubbles will be present at cooler temperatures, even if the system is in perfect condition. If a few bubbles appear at warm temperatures, the system has probably leaked

slightly and should be tested and recharged. If the glass shows severe bubbling or remains completely clear throughout the test, the refrigerant charge may be low, and unit operation should be discontinued immediately after making the test in F. If the sight glass foamed and then remained clear, go on to G.

F. Check the Temperature of the Lines.

Feel along the small, liquid line that runs from the condenser to the expansion valve. This line should be warm along its entire length. If there is a sudden drop in temperature before reaching the expansion valve, the line is clogged at the point where the temperature changes. The line will have to be removed and cleaned by a professional refrigeration mechanic. If the temperature drop occurs at the receiver-drier, this unit will have to be replaced because of saturation with moisture or dirt.

While the liquid line between the condenser and the expansion valve is the most common location for clogging, a sudden drop in temperature in the condenser or in the compressor discharge line will also indicate clogging. Be careful when feeling either the line between the compressor and condenser, or the condenser itself, as the temperature may be very high.

If the compressor discharge and suction lines are at about the same temperature and the sight glass does not foam even at start up, the entire refrigerant charge has probably leaked out.

G. Check System Performance and Blower Operation.

Operate the system with the blower at high speed and the temperature control set at the lowest setting. The engine should be operated at a fast idle (over 1,100 rpm).

The temperature at the discharge ducts varies with the weather and other conditions. However, most systems will maintain a comfortable temperature in all but the most extreme weather. If the temperature exceeds 90° F, a slight reduction in performance may be expected.

If system performance is inadequate, the problem may be in the blower, refrigeration system, or temperature control system.

If the blower operates on all speeds and changes its speed every time the blower speed switch is moved, it is probably operating properly. If it operates only on one or two of the positions, the blower resistor may be at fault. This resistor is usually located in the engine compartment on the evaporator housing. Remove the resistor and check it for burned or shorted resistor coils. If there is any evidence of burning, separation, or bending of the coils, replace the resistor.

If the blower does not operate at all, run a jumper wire from the battery positive terminal to the blower motor terminal to see if the motor will operate. If it does not run, check the ground strap. If the ground is all right, replace the blower motor. If the blower operates, check each connection between the motor and the air conditioning switch to isolate the faulty wire or connection.

If the system output is inadequate, even though the blower operates properly, the temperature control system may be at fault. Have someone move the temperature control lever back and forth while you look under the hood and dash for a moving control cable. The cable operates either an air mixing door or a water valve. If no cable movement is apparent and shifting the temperature control back and forth has a direct effect on the operation of the compressor, have the thermostatic switch checked by a professional air conditioning mechanic.

If the temperature control lever is moving a water valve or air door linkage, inspect the linkage to see that it is operating properly. The most common problem is an improper adjustment or slipping adjusting screw. The adjustment is usually made on

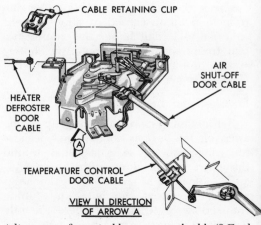

Adjustment of a typical heater control cable (© Ford Motor Co)

the clamp which holds the cable in place. Adjust the cable's position so that the door or water valve will move to the fully closed or maximum cooling position just before the temperature control reaches the full cold setting. Where a vacuum-operated water valve is used to stop coolant flow through the heater core at maximum cooling only, check the vacuum line to the valve. If the vacuum line is not cracked and is tightly connected to the valve, have the valve checked by a professional. Otherwise, replace or tighten the line as necessary.

If the air conditioner performs satisfactorily for 20–40 minutes and then begins to perform less efficiently, the evaporator core is freezing. The suction throttling valve or de-icing switch is malfunctioning. Have a professional air conditioning man adjust or repair the unit.

11 · Manual Transmission and Clutch

How They Work

Because of the way the gasoline engine breathes, it can produce torque, or twisting force, only within a narrow speed range. Most modern engines must turn at about 2,500 rpm to produce their peak torque. By 4,500 rpm they are producing so little torque that continued increases in engine speed produce no power increases.

The transmission and clutch are employed to vary the relationship between engine speed and the speed of the wheels so that adequate engine power can be produced under all circumstances. The clutch

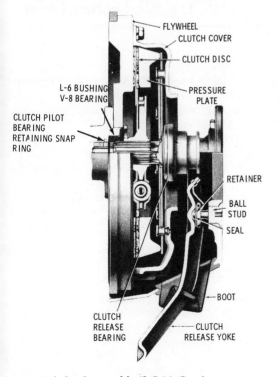

L-6 BUSHING
V-8 BEARING

CLUTCH PILOT
BEARING
RETAINING SNAP
RING

FLYWHEEL
CLUTCH COVER
CLUTCH DISC
PRESSURE
PLATE

RETAINER
BALL
STUD
SEAL
BOOT

CLUTCH
RELEASE
BEARING
CLUTCH
RELEASE YOKE

A typical clutch assembly (© G.M. Corp)

allows engine torque to be applied to the transmission input shaft gradually, due to mechanical slippage. The car can, consequently, be started smoothly from a full stop.

The transmission changes the ratio between the rotating speeds of the engine and the wheels by the use of gears. Three-speed or four-speed transmissions are most common. The lower gears allow full engine power to be applied to the rear wheels during acceleration at low speeds.

The clutch driven plate is a thin disc, the center of which is splined to the transmission input shaft. Both sides of the disc are covered with a layer of material which is similar to brake lining and which is capable of allowing slippage without roughness or excessive noise.

The clutch cover is bolted to the engine flywheel and incorporates a diaphragm spring which provides the pressure to engage the clutch. The cover also houses the pressure plate. The driven disc is sandwiched between the pressure plate and the smooth surface of the flywheel when the clutch pedal is released, thus forcing it to turn at the same speed as the engine crankshaft.

The transmission contains a mainshaft which passes all the way through the transmission, from the clutch to the driveshaft. This shaft is separated at one point, so that front and rear portions can turn at different speeds.

Power is transmitted by a countershaft in the lower gears and reverse. The gears of the countershaft mesh with gears on the mainshaft, allowing power to be carried from one to the other. All the countershaft gears are integral with that shaft, while several of the mainshaft gears can either rotate independently of the shaft or be locked to it. Shifting from one gear to the

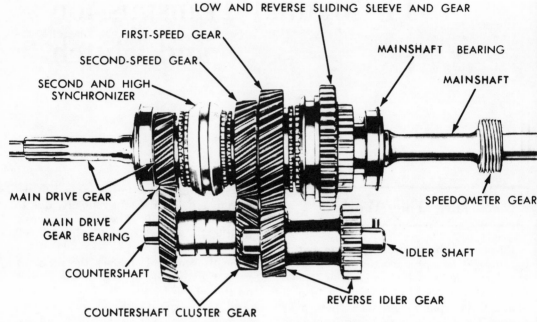

LOW AND REVERSE SLIDING SLEEVE AND GEAR

FIRST-SPEED GEAR

SECOND-SPEED GEAR

SECOND AND HIGH
SYNCHRONIZER

MAINSHAFT   BEARING

MAINSHAFT

MAIN DRIVE GEAR

MAIN DRIVE
GEAR   BEARING

SPEEDOMETER GEAR

COUNTERSHAFT

IDLER SHAFT

COUNTERSHAFT CLUSTER GEAR

REVERSE IDLER GEAR

The inner workings of a transmission (© G.M. Corp)

next causes one of the gears to be freed from rotating with the shaft, and locks another to it. Gears are locked and unlocked by internal dog clutches which slide between the center of the gear and the shaft. The forward gears usually employ synchronizers: friction members which smoothly bring gear and shaft to the same speed before the toothed dog clutches are engaged.

The clutch is operating properly if:

1. It will stall the engine when released with the vehicle held stationary.

2. The shift lever can be moved freely between first and reverse gears when the vehicle is stationary and the clutch disengaged.

A clutch pedal free-play adjustment is incorporated in the linkage. If there is about 1–2 in. of motion before the pedal begins to release the clutch, it is adjusted properly. Inadequate free-play wears all parts of the clutch releasing mechanisms and may cause slippage. Excessive free-play may cause inadequate release and hard shifting of gears.

Some clutches use a hydraulic system in place of mechanical linkage. If the clutch fails to release, fill the clutch master cylinder with fluid to the proper level and pump the clutch pedal to fill the system with fluid. Bleed the system in the same way as a brake system. If leaks are located, tighten loose connections or overhaul the master or slave cylinder as necessary.

Clutch Troubleshooting Chart

SLIPPAGE

Insufficient free-play
(Pedal linkage causing constant pressure against release mechanisms.)
Binding pedal linkage
Driven disc covered with oil
Driven disc worn
(This causes a lack of spring tension.)
Spring tension poor due to heat-weakened springs
Pressure plate warped from heat
Driven plate not seated (brand new)
Clutch overheated, due to extreme operating conditions

CLUTCH FAILS TO RELEASE— HARD SHIFTING

Excessive clutch pedal free-play
Clutch plate binding on transmission input shaft
Severely warped driven disc or pressure plate
Transmission input shaft binding in the pilot bearing

CLUTCH ENGAGEMENT ROUGH

Linkage requires lubrication
Worn or loose engine or transmission mounts
Loose clutch cover mounting bolts
Oil on flywheel
Disc hub binding on transmission input shaft
Pressure plate distorted or cracked

CLUTCH NOISY

(Noise occurs constantly)
Insufficient free-play
Worn linkage return spring
(Noise occurs whenever pedal is depressed)
Worn or poorly lubricated throwout bearing

POOR CLUTCH FACING LIFE

Insufficient pedal free-play
Riding the clutch (driving with foot on pedal)
Hard usage
Rough surface on flywheel or pressure plate
Oil or water on facing
Weak pressure plate springs
(causing constant slippage)

Transmission Troubleshooting Chart

JUMPING OUT OF GEAR

Transmission not aligned with clutch housing

Gearshift linkage out of adjustment
Mechanical interference with linkage
Insufficient spring tension on shifter rail plunger
End-play in main shaft
Bent shaft
Bent shifter fork
Synchronizer clutch teeth worn

GEARS DO NOT SYNCHRONIZE

If only high gear synchronizes:
Binding main shaft pilot bearing
Clutch not releasing fully
Improper lubrication
Scored or worn synchronizer cones
If only one lower gear synchronizes:
Worn bearings in that mainshaft gear only

STICKING IN GEAR

Clutch not releasing fully
Binding shifter rail
Burred transmission mainshaft
Frozen synchronizer clutch
Inadequate or improper lubrication
Corroded transmission parts
Defective mainshaft pilot bearing

TRANSMISSION NOISY

Improper or inadequate lubrication
Worn thrust washers in countershaft gear
Loose synchronizer hub spline
Damaged or worn gear teeth
Loose transmission bearings

12 · The Automatic Transmission

How It Works

The automatic transmission allows engine torque and power to be transmitted to the rear wheels within a narrow range of engine operating speeds. The transmission will allow the engine to turn fast enough to produce plenty of power and torque at very low speeds, while keeping it at a sensible rpm at high vehicle speeds. The transmission performs this job entirely without driver assistance.

The transmission uses a light fluid as the medium for the transmission of power. This fluid also works in the operation of various hydraulic control circuits and as a lubricant. Because the transmission fluid performs all of these three functions, trouble within the unit can easily travel from one part to another. For this reason, and because of the complexity and unusual operating principles of the transmission, a very sound understanding of the basic principles of operation will simplify troubleshooting.

THE TORQUE CONVERTER

The torque converter replaces the conventional clutch. It has three functions:

1. It allows the engine to idle with the vehicle at a standstill—even with the transmission in gear.

2. It allows the transmission to shift from range to range smoothly, without requiring that the driver close the throttle during the shift.

3. It multiplies engine torque to an increasing extent as vehicle speed drops and throttle opening is increased. This has the effect of making the transmission more responsive and reduces the amount of shifting required.

The torque converter is a metal case which is shaped like a sphere that has been flattened on opposite sides. It is bolted to the rear end of the engine's crankshaft. Generally, the entire metal

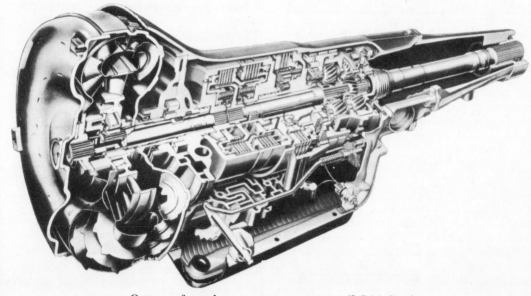

Cutaway of a modern automatic transmission (© G.M. Corp)

86

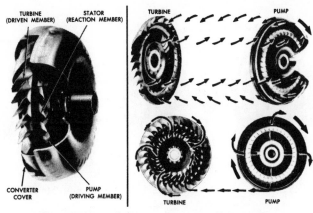

Cutaway view of a torque converter (© G.M. Corp)

case rotates at engine speed and serves as the engine's flywheel.

The case contains three sets of blades. One set is attached directly to the case. This set forms the torus or pump. Another set is directly connected to the output shaft, and forms the turbine. The third set is mounted on a hub which, in turn, is mounted on a stationary shaft through a one-way clutch. This third set is known as the stator.

A pump, which is driven off the transmission input shaft, keeps the torque converter full of transmission fluid at all times. Fluid flows continuously through the unit to provide cooling.

Under low-speed acceleration, the torque converter functions as follows:

The torus is turning faster than the turbine. It picks up fluid at the center of the converter and, through centrifugal force, slings it outward. Since the outer edge of the converter moves faster than the portions at the center, the fluid picks up speed.

The fluid then enters the outer edge of the turbine blades. It then travels back toward the center of the converter case along the turbine blades. In impinging upon the turbine blades, the fluid loses the energy picked up in the torus.

If the fluid were now to immediately be returned directly into the torus, both halves of the converter would have to turn at approximately the same speed at all times, and torque input and output would both be the same.

In flowing through the torus and turbine, the fluid picks up two types of flow, or flow in two separate directions. It flows through the turbine blades, and it spins with the engine. The stator, whose blades are stationary when the vehicle is being accelerated at low speeds, converts one type of flow into another. Instead of allowing the fluid to flow straight back into the torus, the stator's curved blades turn the fluid almost 90° toward the direction of rotation of the engine. Thus the fluid does not flow as fast toward the torus, but is already spinning when the torus picks it up. This has the effect of allowing the torus to turns much faster than the turbine. This difference in speed may be compared to the difference in speed between the smaller and larger gears in any gear train. The result is that engine power output is higher, and engine torque is multiplied.

As the speed of the turbine increases, the fluid spins faster and faster in the direction of engine rotation. As a result, the ability of the stator to redirect the fluid flow is reduced. Under cruising conditions, the stator is eventually forced to rotate on its one-way clutch in the direction of engine rotation. Under these conditions, the torque converter begins to behave almost like a solid shaft, with the torus and turbine speeds being almost equal.

THE PLANETARY GEARBOX

The ability of the torque converter to multiply engine torque is limited. Also, the unit tends to be more efficient when the turbine is rotating at relatively high speeds. Therefore, a planetary gearbox is used to carry the power output of the turbine to the driveshaft to make the most efficient use of the converter.

Planetary gears function very similarly to conventional transmission gears. However, their construction is different in that

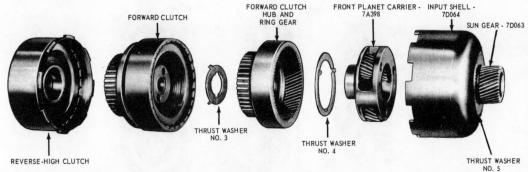

Exploded view of a planetary gearset (Courtesy, Ford Motor Co)

three elements make up one gear system, and in that all three elements are different from one another. The three elements are: an outer gear that is shaped like a hoop, with teeth cut into the inner surface; a sun gear, mounted on a shaft and located at the very center of the outer gear; and a set of three planet gears, held by pins in a ring-like planet carrier and meshing with both the sun gear and the outer gear. Either the outer gear or the sun gear may be held stationary, providing more than one possible torque multiplication factor for each set of gears. Also, if all three gears are forced to rotate at the same speed, the gearset forms, in effect, a solid shaft.

Most modern automatics use the planetary gears to provide either a single reduction ratio of about 1.8:1, or two reduction gears: a low of about 2.5:1, and an intermediate of about 1.5:1. Bands and clutches are used to hold various portions of the gearsets to the transmission case or to the shaft on which they are mounted. Shifting is accomplished, then, by changing the portion of each planetary gearset which is held to the transmission case or to the shaft.

THE SERVOS AND ACCUMULATORS

The servos are hydraulic pistons and cylinders. They resemble the hydraulic actuators used on many familiar machines, such as bulldozers. Hydraulic fluid enters the cylinder, under pressure, and forces the piston to move to engage the band or clutches.

The accumulators are used to cushion the engagement of the servos. The transmission fluid must pass through the accumulator on the way to the servo. The accumulator housing contains a thin piston

which is sprung away from the discharge passage of the accumulator. When fluid passes through the accumulator on the way to the servo, it must move the piston against spring pressure, and this action smooths out the action of the servo.

THE HYDRAULIC CONTROL SYSTEM

The hydraulic pressure used to operate the servos comes from the main transmission oil pump. This fluid is channeled to the various servos through the shift valves. There is generally a manual shift valve which is operated by the transmission selector lever and an automatic shift valve for each automatic upshift the transmission provides: i.e., two-speed automatics have a low-high shift valve, while three-speeds will have a 1–2 valve, and a 2–3 valve.

There are two pressures which effect the operation of these valves. One is the governor pressure which is affected by vehicle speed. The other is the modulator pressure

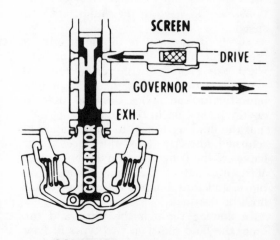

GOVERNOR

Schematic of a governor (© G.M. Corp)

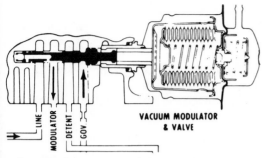

Schematic of a vacuum modulator (© G.M. Corp)

which is affected by intake manifold vacuum or throttle position. Governor pressure rises with an increase in vehicle speed, and modulator pressure rises as the throttle is opened wider. By responding to these two pressures, the shift valves cause the upshift points to be delayed with increased throttle opening to make the best use of the engine's power output.

Most transmissions also make use of an auxiliary circuit for downshifting. This circuit may be actuated by the throttle linkage or the vacuum line which actuates the modulator, or by a cable or solenoid. It applies pressure to a special downshift surface on the shift valve or valves.

The transmission modulator also governs the line pressure, used to actuate the servos. In this way, the clutches and bands will be actuated with a force matching the torque output of the engine.

Automatic Transmission Troubleshooting

A. Check the Transmission Fluid Level.

The transmission fluid level should always be checked first when troubleshooting for transmission slippage or failure to engage either forward or reverse gears. Loss of only a small amount of fluid can cause air to be drawn into the transmission oil pump pick-up. The resultant foaming of the oil prevents proper engagement of the clutches and bands.

Check the fluid as follows:

1. Operate the vehicle for 15 miles or so to bring the transmission to normal operating temperature. If the transmission gears will not engage, add at least enough oil to produce a measurement on the dipstick.

2. Place the selector lever in each of the positions, and then place it in Park.

3. Check the fluid level by removing the dipstick, wiping it, reinserting it, and then removing it for a reading. Make sure the dipstick is all the way in during the final insertion into the transmission. Bring the fluid up to the full mark. If the fluid level is too high, drain fluid from the pan until it is within the proper range. Excess fluid will cause foaming within the transmission. The gears will pick up the fluid and throw it around inside the housing.

If the transmission leaks fluid, the leak should be repaired. Leaks should be detected as follows:

1. Operate the vehicle until the transmission fluid is at operating temperature.

2. Thoroughly remove all oil and grease from the bottom of the transmission.

3. Look for the leak with the engine operating.

4. If no leak is detected with the engine in operation, check again with the engine stopped, after fluid has had a chance to drain back into the transmission sump.

Leaks occur at the seam between the oil pan and transmission case because of improperly torqued pan bolts, a faulty pan gasket, or a gasket mounting face that is rough. The front and rear seals, and all seals where shafts, cables, and filler pipes pass through the case should be checked.

In some cases, leaks are caused by porosity of the transmission case. These leaks may frequently be repaired with epoxy cement.

B. Check the Engine Condition and Linkage Adjustments.

If the transmission shifts are consistently late (at too high a speed) and rough or harsh, and performance is sluggish, the engine may be at fault. An engine which is out of tune, or has mechanical problems such as low compression will suffer reduced torque at high throttle openings and low manifold vacuum levels. Since the transmission measures either manifold vacuum or throttle position in order to determine shift points and line pressure, an abnormal engine condition will affect the transmission. Also, an engine which performs poorly will prevent the torque converter from working at its best, resulting in very poor performance. Make sure that the engine has good compression on all cylinders and is in good tune before condemning the transmission.

An improperly adjusted mechanical linkage to the modulator valve, or an improperly adjusted vacuum modulator can cause late and harsh shifts, or early, sluggish shifts. Vacuum leaks in the manifold or in the line to the vacuum modulator valve can also cause problems.

Factory manuals provide adjustment specifications for mechanical linkages. However, if these specifications are not readily available, the linkage may be adjusted to see if the problem is merely improper adjustment at assembly or last overhaul. Adjust as follows:

1. Examine the linkage to see which way it moves as the engine throttle is opened.

2. Remove the cotter pin or other locking device.

3. Turn the adjustment so that the transmission linkage will move farther in the direction of open throttle for later, harsher shifts, or toward closed throttle for earlier, smoother shifts.

4. Replace the locking device.

Vacuum modulators are adjustable if an adjusting screw protrudes from the cover. Turn the screw inward (clockwise) for earlier, smoother shifts, and outward for later, harsher shifts.

It would be wise to consult the specifications tables provided by the factory regarding proper shift points. Early, smooth shifts can cause premature clutch wear.

C. Check the Torque Converter.

Torque converter problems are usually characterized by either of the following:

1. Low engine rpm at lower speeds, and sluggish acceleration until cruising speeds are reached.

2. Normal performance until cruising conditions are reached, at which time the engine races, and fuel economy is very poor.

The first problem is caused by a slipping stator clutch, while the second results if the clutch is frozen. The first symptom may be checked further by running a stall test according to the manufacturer's instructions. This involves measuring engine revolutions with the transmission in gear, the vehicle stationary, and the throttle wide open. Make sure, if the second symptom is noticed, that the problem is not failure of the transmission to shift into high gear.

Improper stall speed or other torque converter problems can be cured only by replacement of the complete converter unit.

D. The Line Pressure Test.

This test is accomplished by operating the vehicle with a 200 lbs pressure gauge installed in a special fitting in the side of the transmission. A long hose is used with the gauge so it may be read while the mechanic is riding inside the passenger compartment of the car. Most factory manuals have a line pressure chart which lists proper pressure under various operating conditions. Finding whether the line pressure is normal, low, or high helps considerably in troubleshooting internal transmission problems.

Troubleshooting Chart

Consult the chart below to locate various transmission problems.

FAILURE TO UPSHIFT

Low fluid level
Incorrect linkage adjustment
Faulty or sticking governor
Leaking valve body
Leak in vacuum lines to vacuum modulator
Faulty modulator
Stuck shift valve, detent cable, or downshift solenoid
Faulty clutches, servos, or oil pump

FAILURE TO DOWNSHIFT (KICK-DOWN)

Improperly adjusted throttle linkage
Sticking downshift linkage or cable
Faulty modulator
Stuck shift valve
Faulty downshift solenoid or wiring
Faulty detent valve
Faulty clutches or servos

HIGH LINE PRESSURE

Vacuum leak or modulator leak or malfunction

Faulty Pressure Regulator

Improper pressure regulator adjustment
Faulty valve body

Low Line Pressure

Low fluid level
Faulty modulator
Faulty oil pump
Clogged strainer
Faulty seals in accumulators or clutches
Faulty transmission case

Slippage

Low oil level
Low line pressure (see above)
Faulty accumulator seals
Faulty servo piston seals
Clutch plates worn or burned
Incorrect shift linkage adjustment

Noise

Low oil level
Clogged strainer
Faulty oil pump
Water in oil
Valve body malfunction (buzzing)

13 · The Rear Axle

How It Works

The rear axle is a special type of transmission that reduces the speed of the drive from the engine and transmission and divides the power to the rear wheels.

Power enters the rear axle from the driveshaft via the companion flange. The flange is mounted on the drive pinion shaft. The drive pinion shaft and gear which carry the power into the differential turn at engine speed. The gear on the end of the pinion shaft drives a large ring gear the axis of rotation of which is 90° away from that

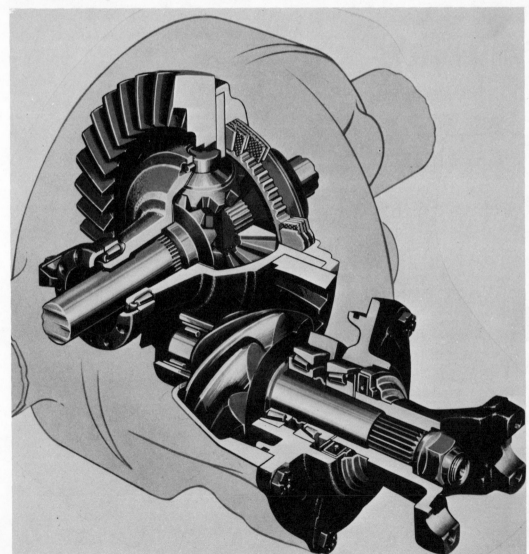

Cutaway of a typical rear axle (© Ford Motor Co)

of the pinion. The pinion and gear reduce the speed and multiply the power by the gear ratio of the axle, and change the direction of rotation to turn the axle shafts which drive both wheels. The rear axle gear ratio is found by dividing the number of pinion gear teeth into the number of ring gear teeth.

The ring gear drives the differential case. The case provides the two mounting points for the ends of a pinion shaft on which are mounted two pinion gears. The pinion gears drive the two side gears, one of which is located on the inner end of each axle shaft.

By driving the axle shafts through this arrangement, the differential allows the outer drive wheel to turn faster than the inner drive wheel in a turn.

The main drive pinion and the side bearings, which bear the weight of the differential case, are shimmed to provide proper bearing preload, and to position the pinion and ring gears properly.

NOTE: *The proper adjustment of the relationship of the ring and pinion gears is critical. It should be attempted only by those with extensive equipment and/or experience.*

Limited-slip differentials include clutches which tend to link each axle shaft to the differential case. Clutches may be engaged either by spring action or by pressure produced by the torque on the axles during a turn. During turning on a dry pavement, the effects of the clutches are overcome, and each wheel turns at the required speed. When slippage occurs at either wheel, however, the clutches will transmit some of the power to the wheel

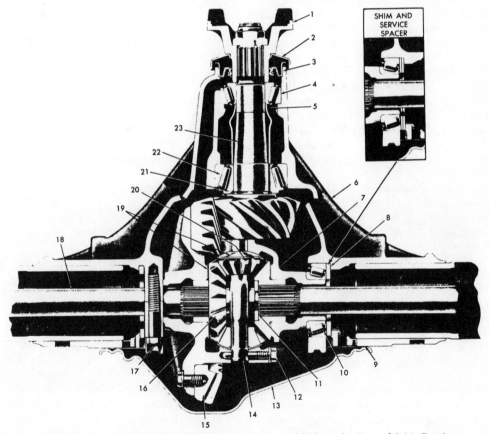

Typical General Motors rear axle—C type (Courtesy of Chevrolet Div. of G.M. Corp)

1. Companion flange	7. Differential case	13. Cover	19. Thrust washer
2. Deflector	8. Shim	14. Pinion shaft	20. Differential pinion
3. Pinion oil seal	9. Gasket	15. Ring gear	21. Shim
4. Pinion front bearing	10. Differential bearing	16. Slide gear	22. Pinion rear bearing
5. Pinion bearing spacer	11. C Lock	17. Bearing cap	23. Drive pinion
6. Differential carrier	12. Pinion shaft lockbolt	18. Axle shaft	

which has the greater amount of traction. Because of the presence of clutches, limited-slip units require a special lubricant. Consult a Chilton Manual or factory information for unit identification and lubricant recommendations.

Diagnosing Noises

To diagnose noises, first warm up the differential thoroughly, and then operate the vehicle on a very smooth, blacktop surface. Note the types of noises produced and the vehicle speeds at which they occur. Then, stop the vehicle and operate the engine at the approximate speeds at which it was turning during the production of noise on the road. If the same noises occur, poor engine, transmission, or exhaust system mounts may be at fault.

If the noises do not recur, pump up the tires to about 50 psi and repeat the test. If the noises recur, the tires are not at fault.

If the tires are not causing the problem, repeat the test, changing the position of the throttle gradually to subject the differential to drive, coast, and overrun conditions. If radical changes are noted, the problem lies in the rear axle gears or bearings.

If the noises occur only while cornering, even if the cornering is fairly gentle, the problem probably lies in the differential side gears or pinions, as these parts work against each other only on turns. Use of the wrong lubricant in limited-slip differentials will produce chattering noises on turns.

Wheel bearing noise will usually diminish slightly when the brakes are applied. A cross-check may be made by jacking up the car and spinning the front wheels to check for noise. Rear wheel bearing noise will usually change as the car is swerved from side to side, while rear axle noises tend to remain constant.

Check all parts of the rear suspension for metal-to-metal contact which might telegraph normal axle noise. Replace any faulty bushings.

Defective bearings in the rear axle generally produce a rough noise that is constant in pitch, while gearing problems generally produce a noise that cycles and varies in pitch with the speed.

Gear noises can frequently be caused by low lubricant level or improperly adjusted ring and pinion gears.

Troubleshooting Chart

Noises

Inadequate amount of lubricant
Improper lubricant
Wheels loose on drums
Improper ring gear and pinion adjustment
Excessively worn ring and pinion gear teeth
Drive bearing preload improperly adjusted
Differential bearing preload improperly adjusted
Loose companion flange (flange should be turned 90° before tightening)
Worn pinion shaft
Worn keyways or splines in axle shafts

Leakage

Excessive fluid
Clogged vent
Loose housing bolts or cover screws
Worn drive pinion oil seal (may be caused by a rough companion flange)
Worn axle shaft oil seals
Cracked housing

Overheating

Insufficient lubricant
Too light a lubricant in use
Bearings adjusted too tightly
Insufficient ring-to-pinion clearance
Gears very badly worn

Wheels Fight Each Other on Turns (Limited-Slip)

Use of too light a lubricant

Only One Wheel Spins (Limited-Slip)

Use of too heavy a lubricant
Worn clutches
Clutches improperly assembled

DIAGNOSING DRIVESHAFT AND UNIVERSAL JOINT NOISES

Install a tachometer on the vehicle and operate it at the speed at which vibration occurs. Then slow the vehicle and shift it to a lower gear. Operate the vehicle at the same engine speed at which the vibration occurs in high gear.

If the vibration recurs, it is in the transmission or engine. If it does not appear, or is at a much lower frequency, it is in the drive line.

Driveshaft and Universal Joint Troubleshooting Chart

VIBRATION

Undercoating on driveshaft
Missing balance weights

Loose U-joint flange bolts
Worn U-joints
Excessive U-joint bolt torque
Excessively tight U-joints
Damaged companion flange
Drive shaft or companion flange unbalanced
Incorrect rear joint angle due to improper riding height or other rear suspension defects

NOISES

Worn U-joints
Loose companion flange
Loose control arm bushing (coil type rear springs)

14 · The Front Suspension and Wheel Alignment

How the Front Suspension Works

Most front suspensions include two control arms (an upper and a lower) which are attached to the chassis by hinges. The hinges permit the outer ends of the control arms to move up and down in relation to the chassis as the vehicle travels over bumps in the road surface, while keeping the outer ends from moving forward or backward.

The outer ends of the control arms are kept an equal distance apart by steering knuckles. The steering knuckles are held in place, at top and bottom, by ball joints. The wheel spindles extend outward from about the middle of the steering knuckles. The ball joints permit the upward and downward motion of the steering knuckles and the turning motion required for cornering, while keeping them vertical. Tie rods link them to the steering gear.

The upper and lower ends of the steering knuckles are not the same distance from the chassis; the upper end is closer. Therefore, the wheel spindles tend to angle downward and lift the vehicle slightly whenever the wheels are not pointed straight ahead.

A list of various terms used in wheel alignment, with their definitions, follows.

Camber

The wheel is not positioned vertically on most vehicles, but is angled so that the upper edge is further away from the chassis than is the lower edge. Angling the wheel in this manner makes better use of the tire tread during cornering.

Caster

The vehicle has caster if the upper end of the steering knuckle is positioned slightly behind the lower end. Caster helps the vehicle's steering return to the

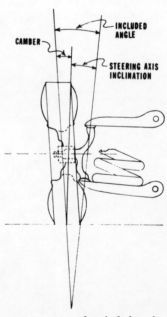

Camber, steering axis and included angle

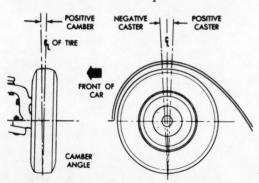

Caster and Camber angles

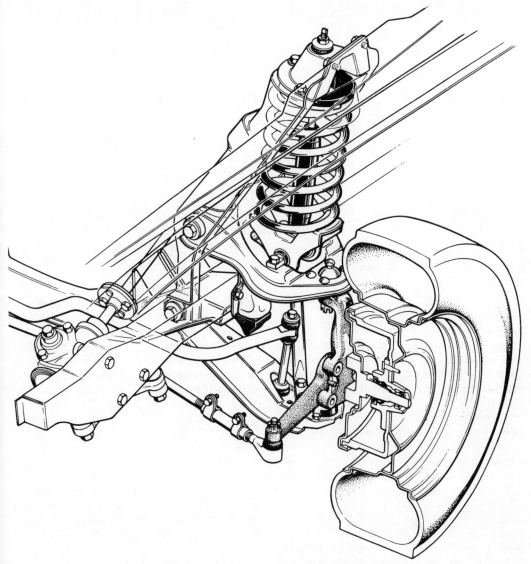

A typical front suspension system (© Ford Motor Co)

straight-ahead position, and improves directional stability.

Steering Axis Inclination

Steering axis inclination results from the fact that the upper end of the steering knuckle is closer to the chassis than the lower end. This angular mounting is what causes the vehicle to lift slightly during cornering. The car's weight thus tends to help the steering return to the center and to aid directional stability.

Included Angle

The included angle is the sum of the steering axis inclination and the caster an-

gles. It is the angle between a line drawn between the two mounting points of the steering knuckle and a line drawn vertically through the center of the wheel.

In each of the above definitions, an imaginary angle between the vertical and the centerline of the wheel or the steering knuckle is described. On an alignment chart, these angles are referred to in degrees of positive caster, camber, etc. If the angle is listed as zero, the unit in question is to be perfectly vertical. If a figure of less than zero is listed, the unit should be angled in the opposite direction. For example, negative caster refers to an adjustment which positions the upper end of the steer-

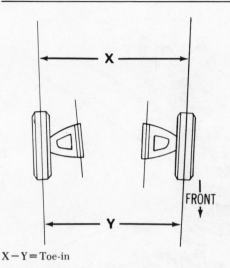

X − Y = Toe-in

ing knuckle ahead of the lower end, rather than behind.

Toe-In

On most vehicles, when the front wheels are stationary, they are closer together at the front than at the rear. Aligning the wheels in this manner compensates for various frictional forces that alter the angles between the wheels when the vehicle is moving. Thus, the wheels are brought into a parallel position, relative to each other, as the vehicle gains speed. Toe-in is measured in inches; the difference between the distance separating the front and rear centerlines of the wheels.

Toe-Out

The steering is designed so that the inner wheel turns more sharply toward the center of the turn than the outer wheel turns. This compensates for the fact that

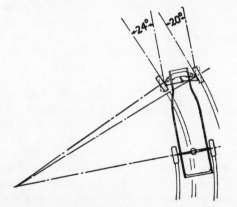

Toe-out. Inside wheel turns a greater number of degrees

the inner wheel actually travels a shorter distance during the turn. Designing the steering in this manner avoids having the front wheels fight each other, thus improving tire life and aiding stability. Where toe-out is to be checked, angles are given for the inner and outer wheel relative to travel in a straight line. Thus, in a left-hand turn, the left (inner) wheel might be 24° from straight ahead, and the right (outer) wheel 20° from straight ahead. For a right turn, the figures would be reversed.

Tracking

During straight-line operation, the vehicle's rear wheels must duplicate, or run parallel to, the paths of the front wheels. To measure the accuracy of a vehicle's tracking, measure the distance from the right-side lower ball joint to a point on the left side of the rear axle, and repeat the measurement for the left-side lower ball joint and a similar point on the right side of the rear axle. You may wish to drop a plumb line from each of these four points to the ground and mark the spots in order to avoid interference from various parts of the vehicle's undercarriage. The two diagonal lines should be equal in length to within 1/4 in. Otherwise, the frame of the vehicle is bent or the rear axle is off center.

The rear wheels may also be checked for toe-in or toe-out by measuring between the inner surfaces of the tires at front and rear. Toe-in or toe-out in excess of manufacturer's specifications indicates a bent rear axle.

There is a special machine designed to check the alignment of the front wheels. Caster is first adjusted to specifications by moving the upper control arm. This may be accomplished by repositioning shims, changing the length of a strut with adjusting nuts, or by repositioning the mounting point of a strut on the frame. Camber is then accomplished by pulling the entire control arm toward the frame or forcing it further away. This involves repositioning shims equally at the front and rear of the control arm, turning adjusting nuts an equal amount, or repositioning a strut.

There are exceptions to these general rules. For example, on 1965–66 Thunderbirds, these adjustments affect the lower control arm, and on Vegas, camber is adjusted before caster. Consult a manual for

Caster and camber adjusting shim installation (Courtesy of Chevrolet Div. of G.M. Corp)

the precise method to be used for the vehicle in question.

On all vehicles, toe-in is adjusted after caster and camber are correct by turning the adjusting sleeves on the tie rods. These sleeves should be turned in equal amounts in opposite directions in order to keep the steering wheel centered. If the wheel is off center, it may be centered without affecting toe-in by turning both adjusting sleeves in the same direction.

When caster, camber, and toe-in have been adjusted, steering axis inclination and toe-out figures should be correct. If not, a worn ball joint or bent suspension or steering part is at fault.

Alignment Troubleshooting Chart

Front Wheel Shimmy

1. Tire inflation uneven or low
2. Tires improperly mounted or wheels improperly balanced
3. Incorrect caster
4. Incorrect toe-in
5. Uneven tire wear

6. Excessively worn wheel bearings
7. Worn ball joints
8. Bent steering knuckle(s)
9. Inoperative shock absorbers

Excessive Tire Wear

1. Both edges wear: insufficient pressure
2. Center wears: excessive pressure
3. One edge wears evenly: incorrect camber or toe-in, or damaged suspension parts
4. One edge wears unevenly: incorrect camber or toe-in, insufficient pressure, improper wheel balance, or loose steering linkage
5. Unequal wear between tires: unequal pressures or tire size, incorrect camber or toe-in, loose or bent steering linkage

Vehicle Wanders

1. Tire pressures incorrect or unequal
2. Incorrect caster, camber, or toe-in
3. Loose or worn bushings anywhere in front suspension
4. Rear axle position improper or frame bent
5. Badly worn shock absorbers

Car Pulls to one Side

1. Uneven tire pressures
2. Incorrect caster, camber, or toe-in
3. Brakes improperly adjusted
4. Wheel bearings improperly adjusted
5. Bent steering knuckle or other suspension component
6. Improper tracking

Hard Steering

1. Low tire pressures
2. Inadequate front-end lubrication
3. Incorrect caster
4. Improper steering gear adjustment
5. Sagging front spring

Checking Ball Joints

Support the car as follows:
If the front spring or torsion bar is supported by the lower control arm, locate the jackstand under the lower control arm. Otherwise, support the vehicle by the cross-member or frame.

The ball joint which supports the load should permit a very slight up-and-down motion, and radial play of about ¼ in. Otherwise it should be replaced. The unloaded ball joint should not have any perceptible play at all.

Rear Suspension Alignment

Tracking of the rear wheels should be checked for cars with solid rear axles as described above. These vehicles will have rear wheel alignment problems only rarely, as the rear axle assembly can be bent only by a severe collision.

Corvettes, however, employ a fully independent type of rear suspension which requires setting of the camber and toe-in. The camber is set by adjusting the position of an eccentric cam and bolt located at the inboard mounting of the suspension strut rod.

The toe-in is adjusted by shimming the torque control arm pivot bushing. The shims are inserted on both sides of the bushing inside the frame side member.

15 · Brakes

Hydraulic Systems

Hydraulic systems are used to actuate the brakes of all modern automobiles. The system transports the power required to force the frictional surfaces of the braking system together from the pedal to the individual brake units at each wheel. A hydraulic system is used for two reasons. First, fluid under pressure can be carried to all parts of an automobile by small hoses—some of which are flexible—without taking up a significant amount of room or posing routing problems. Second, a great mechanical advantage can be given to the brake pedal end of the system, and the foot pressure required to actuate the brakes can be reduced by making the surface area of the master cylinder pistons smaller than that of any of the pistons in the wheel cylinders or calipers.

The master cylinder consists of a fluid reservoir and either a single or double cylinder and piston assembly. Double type master cylinders are designed to separate the front and rear braking systems hydraulically in case of a leak.

Steel lines carry the brake fluid to a point on the vehicle's frame near each of the vehicle's wheels. The fluid is then carried to the slave cylinders by flexible tubes in order to allow for suspension and steering movements.

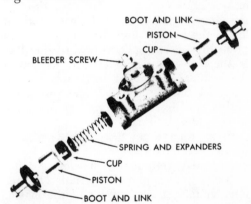

Wheel cylinder (Courtesy of Chevrolet Div. of G.M. Corp)

In drum brake systems, the slave cylinders are called wheel cylinders. Each wheel cylinder contains two pistons, one at either end, which push outward in opposite directions. In disc brake systems, the slave cylinders are part of the calipers. One or four cylinders are used to force the brake pads against the disc, but all cylinders contain one piston only. All slave cylinder pistons employ some type of seal, usually made of rubber, to minimize the leakage of fluid around the piston. A rubber dust boot seals the outer end of the cylinder against dust and dirt. The boot fits around the outer end of the piston on disc brake calipers, and around the brake actuating rod on wheel cylinders.

The hydraulic system operates as fol-

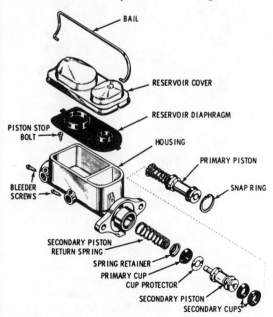

Bendix dual master cylinder (Courtesy of Oldsmobile Div. of G.M. Corp)

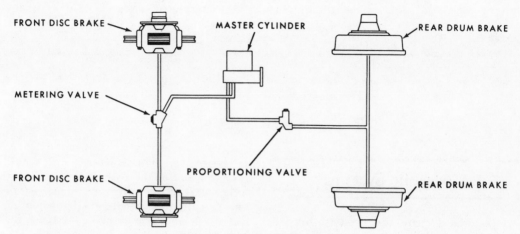

FRONT DISC BRAKE

MASTER CYLINDER

REAR DRUM BRAKE

METERING VALVE

FRONT DISC BRAKE

PROPORTIONING VALVE

REAR DRUM BRAKE

Disc brake hydraulic system

lows: When at rest, the entire system, from the piston(s) in the master cylinder to those in the wheel cylinders or calipers, is full of brake fluid. Upon application of the brake pedal, fluid trapped in front of the master cylinder piston(s) is forced through the lines to the slave cylinders. Here, it forces the pistons outward, in the case of drum brakes, and inward toward the disc, in the case of disc brakes. The motion of the pistons is opposed by return springs mounted outside the cylinders in drum brakes, and by internal springs or spring seals, in disc brakes.

Upon release of the brake pedal, a spring located inside the master cylinder immediately returns the master cylinder piston(s) to the normal position. The pistons contain check valves and the master cylinder has compensating ports drilled in it. These are uncovered as the pistons reach their normal position. The piston check valves allow fluid to flow toward the wheel cylinders or calipers as the pistons withdraw. Then, as the return springs force the brake pads or shoes into the released position, the excess fluid returns to the master cylinder fluid reservoir through the compensating ports. It is during the time the pedal is in the released position that any fluid that has leaked out of the system will be replaced through the compensating ports.

Dual circuit master cylinders employ two pistons, located one behind the other, in the same cylinder. The primary piston is actuated directly by mechanical linkage from the brake pedal. The secondary piston is actuated by fluid trapped between the two pistons. If a leak develops in front of the secondary piston, it moves forward until it bottoms against the front of the master cylinder, and the fluid trapped between the pistons will operate the rear brakes. If the rear brakes develop a leak, the primary piston will move forward until direct contact with the secondary piston takes place, and it will force the secondary piston to actuate the front brakes. In either case, the brake pedal moves farther when the brakes are applied, and less braking power is available.

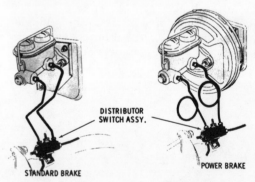

DISTRIBUTOR
SWITCH ASSY.

STANDARD BRAKE

POWER BRAKE

A typical distributor switch assembly (Courtesy, G.M. Corp)

All dual-circuit systems use a distributor switch to warn the driver when only half of the brake system is operational. This switch is located in a valve body which is mounted on the firewall or the frame below the master cylinder. A hydraulic piston receives pressure from both circuits, each circuit's pressure being applied to one end of the piston. When the pressures are in balance, the piston remains stationary. When one circuit has a leak, however, the greater pressure in that circuit during application of the brakes will push the piston to one side, closing the distributor switch and activating the brake warning light.

In disc brake systems, this valve body also contains a metering valve and, in some cases, a proportioning valve. The metering valve keeps pressure from traveling to the disc brakes on the front wheels until the brake shoes on the rear wheels have contacted the drums, ensuring that the front brakes will never be used alone. The proportioning valve throttles the pressure to the rear brakes so as to avoid rear wheel lock-up during very hard braking.

These valves may be tested by removing the lines to the front and rear brake systems and installing special brake pressure testing gauges. Front and rear system pressures are then compared as the pedal is gradually depressed. Specifications vary with the manufacturer and design of the brake system.

Brake system warning lights may be tested by depressing the brake pedal and holding it while opening one of the wheel cylinder bleeder screws. If this does not cause the light to go on, substitute a new lamp, make continuity checks, and, finally, replace the switch as necessary.

The hydraulic system may be checked for leaks by applying pressure to the pedal gradually and steadily. If the pedal sinks very slowly to the floor, the system has a leak. This is not to be confused with a springy or spongy feel due to the compression of air within the lines. If the system leaks, there will be a gradual change in the position of the pedal with a constant pressure.

Check for leaks along all lines and at wheel cylinders. If no external leaks are apparent, the problem is inside the master cylinder.

Hydraulic System Troubleshooting Chart

Low Pedal

1. Brake fluid level low
(If fluid is low, check all lines and wheel cylinders for leaks, and repair as necessary.)
2. Air in system

(This will be accompanied by a spongy feel at the pedal, and by a low fluid level. Check as above.)
3. Master cylinder primary cup damaged, or cylinder bore worn or corroded
4. Use of improper fluid
(Fluid boils from the heat and the resulting gas compresses during pedal application.)

Spongy Pedal

1. Air trapped in system
(This may include the master cylinder. Check for leaks as described above.)
2. Use of improper fluid
3. Clogged compensating port in master cylinder
(This may be checked for by watching for motion of fluid in master cylinder fluid reservoir during early part of brake pedal stroke. If no fluid motion, the port is clogged.)
4. Hoses soft
(Expanding under pressure.)

One Wheel Drags

1. Wheel cylinder piston cups swollen
2. Clogged line

All Brakes Drag

1. Clogged compensating port in master cylinder
2. Mineral oil in system

High Pedal Pressure Required

1. Corroded wheel cylinder
2. Clogged line
3. Clogged compensating port in master cylinder

Power Brake Boosters

Power brakes operate just as standard brake systems except in the actuation of the master cylinder pistons. A vacuum diaphragm is located on the front of the master cylinder and assists the driver in applying the brakes, reducing both the effort and travel he must put into moving the brake pedal.

The vacuum diaphragm housing is connected to the intake manifold by a vacuum hose. A check valve is placed at the point where the hose enters the diaphragm hous-

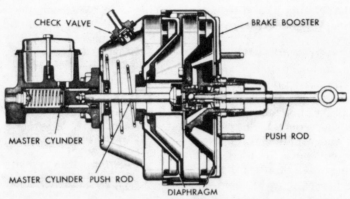

CHECK VALVE

BRAKE BOOSTER

MASTER CYLINDER

PUSH ROD

MASTER CYLINDER PUSH ROD

DIAPHRAGM

Cutaway view of brake booster and master cylinder (© G.M. Corp)

ing, so that during periods of low manifold vacuum brake assist vacuum will not be lost.

Depressing the brake pedal closes off the vacuum source and allows atmospheric pressure to enter on one side of the diaphragm. This causes the master cylinder pistons to move and apply the brakes. When the brake pedal is released, vacuum is applied to both sides of the diaphragm, and return springs return the diaphragm and master cylinder pistons to the released position. If the vacuum fails, the brake pedal rod will butt against the end of the master cylinder actuating rod, and direct mechanical application will occur as the pedal is depressed.

The hydraulic and mechanical problems that apply to conventional brake systems also apply to power brakes, and should be checked for if the tests and chart below do not reveal the problem.

Test for a system vacuum leak as described below:

1. Operate the engine at idle with the transmission in Neutral without touching the brake pedal for at least one minute.

2. Turn off the engine, and wait one minute.

3. Test for the presence of assist vacuum by depressing the brake pedal and releasing it several times. Light application will produce less and less pedal travel, if vacuum was present. If there is no vacuum, air is leaking into the system somewhere.

Test for system operation as follows:

1. Pump the brake pedal (with engine off) until the supply vacuum is entirely gone.

2. Put a light, steady pressure on the pedal.

3. Start the engine, and operate it at idle with the transmission in Neutral. If the system is operating, the brake pedal should fall toward the floor if constant pressure is maintained on the pedal.

Power brake systems may be tested for hydraulic leaks just as ordinary systems are tested, except that the engine should be idling with the transmission in Neutral throughout the test.

Power Brake Booster Troubleshooting Chart

Hard Pedal

1. Faulty vacuum check valve
2. Vacuum hose kinked, collapsed, plugged, leaky, or improperly connected
3. Internal leak in unit
4. Damaged vacuum cylinder
5. Damaged valve plunger
6. Broken or faulty springs
7. Broken plunger stem

Grabbing Brakes

1. Damaged vacuum cylinder
2. Faulty vacuum check valve
3. Vacuum hose leaky or improperly connected
4. Broken plunger stem

Pedal Goes to Floor

Generally, when this problem occurs, it is not caused by the power brake booster. In rare cases, a broken plunger stem may be at fault.

Brake Mechanical Problems

Drum brakes employ two brake shoes mounted on a stationary backing plate to force the brake linings against the inside of the drum which rotates with the wheel. The shoes are held in place by springs; this allows them to slide toward the drums while keeping the linings and drums in alignment. The wheel cylinder's two actuating links force the tops of the shoes outward toward the inner surface of the drum. This action forces the bottoms of the two shoes to contact either end of the adjusting screw. When pressure within the wheel cylinder is relaxed, return springs pull the shoes back, away from the drum.

Most modern drum type brakes are designed to adjust themselves during application when the vehicle is moving in reverse. This motion causes both shoes to rotate very slightly with the drum, rocks an adjusting lever, and thus causes rotation of the adjusting screw by means of a star wheel.

Generally, the rear drum type brakes are used in parking. Cables link the pedal or lever in the passenger compartment to the actuating mechanism inside the drum. Generally, this consists of a lever and strut combination that forces one of the linings outward at the top. This action forces the other lining to contact the drum via the adjusting screw.

Disc brakes employ a double-walled disc rotating with the wheel in place of the drum. The two walls of the disc are

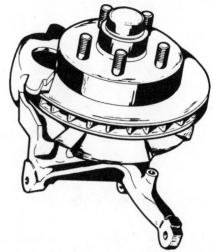

The disc brake (© G.M. Corp)

separated by struts which allow cooling air to flow between them. This superior cooling combined with the fact that the disc does not tend to warp away from the brake pads as drums do, makes the disc brake superior in terms of fade resistance.

The brake pads (linings) used with disc brakes are forced against either side of the disc in a squeezing action by a brake caliper. The caliper may employ only one piston and slide along mounting bushings in order to squeeze the two brake pads against the disc. Or, it may employ a movable piston or pistons on either side of the disc. In this design, the caliper is fixed in place by its mounting bolts.

Disc brakes are inherently self-adjusting. After each application, the pad is pulled away from the disc only far enough to ensure that the brakes do not drag. Thus, the

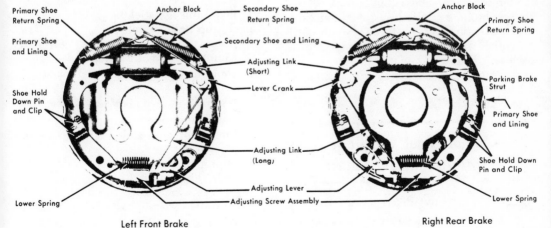

Wagner compound self-adjusting brake (Courtesy of American Motors Corp)

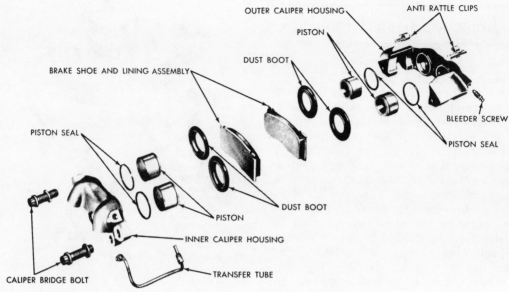

Kelsey-Hayes four piston disc brake (© G.M. Corp)

released position of the piston is continuously adjusted as the pad lining wears.

Parking brakes generally do not require adjustment if the automatic adjusters are working properly. If adjustment is required, proceed as follows:

1. Put the vehicle on a lift so neither rear wheel is touching the ground.

2. Engage the parking brake about halfway.

3. Loosen the locknut on the equalizer yoke, located under the ear, and then turn the adjusting nut just until a drag can be felt on both rear wheels.

4. Release the brake and check for free rotation of the rear wheels.

On systems where a floor-mounted handlever is used, the adjustment is usually contained under the rubber boot which covers the base of the lever. Tighten each of the adjusting nuts on these systems until an equal, slight torque is required to turn each rear drum.

Mechanical Problem Troubleshooting Chart

Low Pedal

1. Automatic adjusters not working, or brakes improperly adjusted

2. Linings or pads excessively worn
3. Drums excessively worn

Spongy Pedal

1. Brake drums too thin
2. Brakes improperly adjusted
3. Brake shoes bent

One Wheel Drags

1. Parking brake improperly adjusted
2. Shoe return springs weak
3. Brakes improperly adjusted
4. Loose front wheel bearings
5. Shoe pads rough or grooved
6. Support plate loose or worn
7. Corroded automatic adjuster parts

All Wheels Drag

1. Pedal linkage sticking
(Check stop light switch.)
2. Automatic adjuster parts corroded
3. Linings or pads distorted
4. Shoes and pads rough or grooved

High Pedal Pressure Required

1. Brakes improperly adjusted
2. Linings or pads soiled with grease or oil
3. Improper linings in use
4. Pedal linkage binding

Car Pulls to One Side

1. Brake shoes or pads of unequal quality, or unequally worn, installed

2. Shoes or pads on one side soiled with grease or oil
3. Caliper loose
4. Linings or drums charred or scored
5. Tire pressures unequal
6. Improper alignment

Noise

1. Linings not fully broken in
2. Disc with excessive lateral run-out
3. Disc imperfectly cast
4. Use of improper lining or pad

Power Steering

Power steering units are mechanical steering gear units incorporating a power assist. A worm shaft, which is rotated by the shaft coming down from the steering wheel via a flexible coupling, causes a rack piston nut to slide up and down inside the housing. This motion is changed into rotating force by the action of an output shaft sector gear. The rack piston nut is forced up and down inside the housing by the ro-

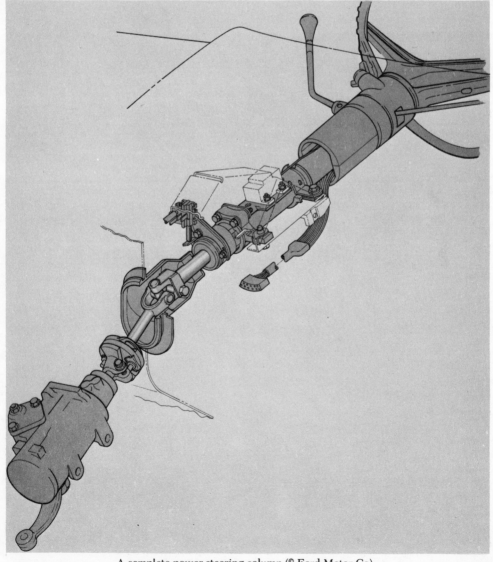

A complete power steering column (© Ford Motor Co)

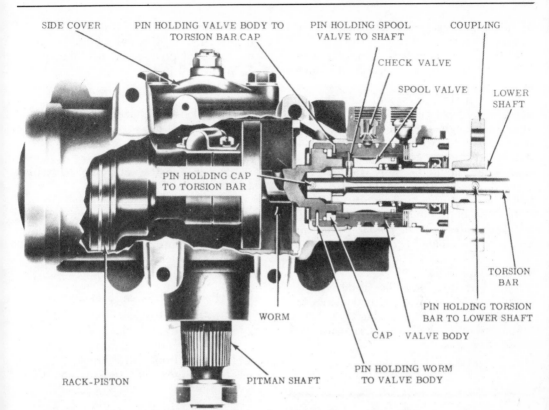

SIDE COVER   PIN HOLDING VALVE BODY TO   PIN HOLDING SPOOL   COUPLING
TORSION BAR CAP   VALVE TO SHAFT

CHECK VALVE

SPOOL VALVE   LOWER
SHAFT

PIN HOLDING CAP
TO TORSION BAR

TORSION
BAR

PIN HOLDING TORSION
BAR TO LOWER SHAFT

WORM   CAP   VALVE BODY

RACK-PISTON   PITMAN SHAFT   PIN HOLDING WORM
TO VALVE BODY

A typical power steering unit (© Ford Motor Co)

tation of the worm gear, which forces the nut to move through the action of recirculating balls. The nut fits tightly inside the housing, and is sealed against the sides of the housing by a ring type seal. Power assist is provided by forcing hydraulic fluid into the housing on one side or the other of the rack piston nut.

The hydraulic pressure is supplied by a rotary vane pump, driven by the engine via V belts. The pump incorporates a flow control valve that bypasses the right amount of fluid for the proper operating pressure. The pump contains a fluid reservoir, located above the main body of the pump. The same fluid lubricates all parts of the power steering unit.

A rotary valve, spool valve, or pivot lever, located in the steering box, senses the rotation of the steering wheel and channels fluid to the upper or lower surface of the rack piston nut.

When power steering problems occur, the pump fluid level should first be checked. Note that two levels are given. The lower level is correct if the pump and fluid are at room temperature, after having been inoperative for some time. The upper level is correct if the system has been in operation (about 175°).

The drive belt should also be checked for looseness, cracks, or glazing. Replace the belt if it is damaged, or tighten it if necessary.

A quick check of the power steering pump oil pressure relief valves may be made by turning the wheel to either stop. There should be a buzzing or swishing noise caused by flow of fluid through bypass valves.

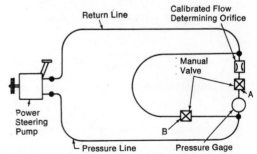

Power Steering pump test circuit diagram (Courtesy of Ford Motor Co)

If steering is difficult, the power steering pump pressure may be tested. A special set of valves and gauges is required. Perform the test as follows:

1. With the engine off, remove the two hoses at the pump and install the gauges and valves.

2. Open both valves, and then start the engine and operate it at idle. The fluid must be brought up to 165–170° F. Closing valve B to build up 350 lbs pressure will speed the process.

3. When the fluid is fully warmed, close valve B. The pressure should be 620 psi or more, or else the pump is faulty.

4. Close both valve A and valve B. *Do not keep valves closed for more than five seconds.* This should raise the pressure level to the manufacturer's specifications for this type of test.

This test measures the ability of the pump to produce pressure. It does not test the pump's pressure regulating valve, a malfunction of which can also cause lack of steering assist.

Power Steering Troubleshooting Chart

HARD STEERING

1. Improper (low) tire pressure
2. Loose or glazed pump drive belt
3. Low fluid level
4. Poorly lubricated front-end parts
5. Bind in steering column
6. Inadequate pump output pressure, due to worn pump parts or malfunctioning pressure regulator valve
7. Obstructions in pump lines
8. Excessive caster
9. Cross-shaft adjustment too tight

CAR VEERS TO ONE SIDE

1. Tire pressures or tread wear unequal
2. Improper front-end alignment
3. Improperly adjusted brakes
4. Faulty shock absorbers or springs

CAR WANDERS

1. Tire pressures improper
2. Improper front-end alignment
3. Play in pitman arm
4. Loose wheel bearings

5. Binding in steering linkage
6. Steering unit valve (rotary valve, spool valve, or pivot lever) malfunctioning
7. Worn ball joints

POWER STEERING NOISY

1. Belts loose or glazed
2. Fluid level low
3. Air in system
4. Kinked hydraulic lines
5. Foreign matter clogging hydraulic lines
6. Flow control valve sticking
7. Steering unit valve (rotary valve, spool valve, or pivot lever) worn
8. Worn pump parts
9. Steering gear mountings loose
10. Interference in front end

POOR RETURN OF STEERING

1. Tires overinflated
2. Improper caster adjustment
3. Bind in steering column
4. Improper front-end lubrication
5. Steering gear adjustments too tight

Manual Steering

Manual steering units convert the rotating force of the steering wheel into a slower, higher torque rotation of the pitman arm. The force of the arm is then transmitted to the wheels by tie rods. Generally, a flexible coupling connects the shaft coming down from the steering wheel to the worm shaft of the steering box.

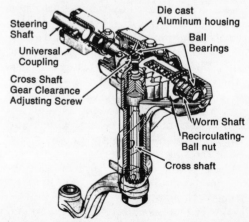

Chrysler steering gear, recirculating ball type (Courtesy of Chrysler Corp)

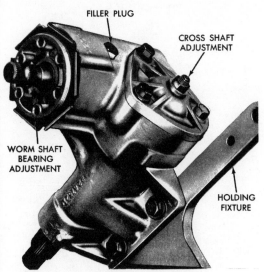

FILLER PLUG

CROSS SHAFT
ADJUSTMENT

WORM SHAFT
BEARING
ADJUSTMENT

HOLDING
FIXTURE

Steering gear adjustment locations (Courtesy of Chrysler Corp)

The worm shaft rotates the cross-shaft or pitman shaft by having the worm gear on the worm shaft rotate the sector gear, mounted on the cross-shaft. In many designs, the efficiency of the unit is increased by using a ball nut incorporating recirculating balls to transmit the rotating force from the worm to the sector gear.

The bearings which carry the worm shaft are usually adjustable, to compensate for wear. In some designs, an adjusting screw is employed, while in others shims may be used to provide the proper bearing preload. Generally, preload is measured by rotating the steering wheel with a spring scale with the pitman arm disconnected from the lower portions of the steering gear.

An adjusting screw is also provided for positioning the cross-shaft for proper meshing of the worm or ball nut and sector gear. After worm bearing preload is adjusted, play is removed from the unit with the cross-shaft adjusting screw, and a recheck of turning effort is made. The adjusting screw must then be backed off slightly if too great a steering wheel turning torque is required. Consult the manufacturer's instructions to make these adjustments because of variations in actual procedures and torque specifications.

Before beginning to troubleshoot manual steering problems, check the condition and pressure of the tires, and the lubrication of the steering gear. Consult the manufacturer's specifications for proper lubricant. It is usually a heavy oil like that used in rear axles. If there is uneven tire wear, it might be wise to align the front end before trying to track down steering malfunctions.

Manual Steering Troubleshooting Chart

HARD STEERING

1. Improper (low) tire pressure
2. Inadequate lubricant
3. Inadequately lubricated front-end parts
4. Bind in steering column
5. Excessive caster
6. Cross-shaft adjustment too tight

CAR VEERS TO ONE SIDE

1. Tire pressures or tread wear unequal
2. Improper front-end alignment
3. Improperly adjusted brakes
4. Faulty shock absorbers or springs

CAR WANDERS

1. Tire pressures improper
2. Improper front-end alignment
3. Play in pitman arm
4. Loose wheel bearings
5. Binding in steering linkage
6. Steering box loose on frame
7. Worn ball joints

POOR RETURN OF STEERING

1. Tires overinflated
2. Improper caster adjustment
3. Bind in steering column
4. Improper front-end lubrication. Steering gear adjustments too tight

17 · Tires

Types of Tires

Bias Ply

Bias ply tires are the most basic and simple design available. The plies of fabric cord which strengthen the tire are applied in a criss-cross fashion for strength. The plies run from rim-edge to rim-edge to help increase the tire's resistance to bruises, and to the forces of braking and cornering.

Belted Bias

These tires are constructed very similarly to the bias-ply tires—with the plies applied in a criss-cross fashion. However, circumferential belts are applied just under the tread to strengthen it and keep it as flat as possible. Thus, the life and performance of the tire are improved. Because the construction is somewhat more complex than that of bias ply tires, belted bias tires are slightly more expensive.

TYPES OF TIRE CONSTRUCTION

Bias-Ply

Belted-Bias

Radial

NOTE: Each tire has an air-tight inner-liner under the body plies. The belted-bias and the radial tires also have under-tread belts, which are shown with a gray tone.

RESULTS OF IMPROPER CARE

Suspension Neglect

Over-Inflation

Under-Inflation

Extreme Cornering

The Firestone Tire & Rubber Company

Radial

Radial tires are the most expensive and best tires made. They offer both improved cornering and improved tread life over belted bias and bias ply tires. The body plies run from rim to rim in a hoop fashion, and the tire employs circumferential belts. The result is that the tread is kept still more perfectly flat and open than with belted bias tires.

There is a relationship between a tire's cornering ability and its ability to provide long tread wear. A tread that remains flat and does not squirm or close up when under heavy load wears more evenly and suffers less from scuffing. Therefore, most manufacturer's recommend that the tire buyer consider purchase of a belted bias or radial tire, claiming that the cost per mile will be lower.

Of course, if the buyer does not plan to keep his car until the new rubber is fully worn out, a less expensive tire should be considered. However, if long mileage is desired, especially under rough cornering or heavy loading conditions, the more expensive designs may prove to be more economical.

If good cornering is desired, the radial is the obvious choice. The cornering characteristics of these tires are so significantly superior to those of other types that mixing radials and other types of tires on the same vehicle is not recommended. The differences in traction between the types can cause undesirable cornering characteristics.

Tire Troubleshooting Chart

Tire Worn in Center of Tread

Overinflation: Excess pressure causes the center of the tread to contact the road, while the edges ride free.

Tire Worn on Outer Edges Only

Underinflation: Underinflation causes the tread to bow, lifting the center off the road. This also increases flexing and heat, and may result in weakening of the tire cords. Note, however, that it is normal for the two sections of tread just one section

from the outer edges to wear more than the others on bias belted tires.

Tires Worn On One Side Only

1. Improper toe-in adjustment: This is the problem if both outer edges or both inner edges are worn
2. Improper camber adjustment.
3. Hard cornering: In addition to wearing the outer edges more than the center, this will round off the edges.

Tires Worn in Several Spots Around the Circumference of the Tread

1. Underinflation combined with improper toe-in adjustment.
2. Improperly balanced tires and wheels.
3. Worn shock absorbers.
4. Worn suspension components.
5. Out-of-round brake drums.

Noises

1. Irregular wear.
2. Low pressure.
3. Bulges due to faulty construction or structural damage.

NOTE: *Inflating tires to 50 pounds pressure for test purposes tends to stop noises. Driving the car on a very smooth road and inflating the tires to a very high pressure, one at a time, will isolate the noisy tire.*

Tire Care

Because the tire employs air under pressure as part of its structure, it is designed around the supporting strength of a gas at a specified pressure. For this reason, running a tire with either too high or too low a pressure actually undermines its structural strength, and, in effect, makes its shape improper for the job to be done.

Not only will improper inflation pressure keep the tread from properly laying on the road, it will reduce the tire's ability to resist damage from road shock. It can also increase operating temperatures.

Tire pressures should, therefore, be carefully checked *at least* once a month. A hand tire gauge of good quality should be used.

In almost all cases, the manufacturer's recommendations for pressures should be followed. While manufacturers tended to recommend low pressures several years ago, in order to achieve good ride characteristics, their recommendations from about 1968 are generally quite accurate. Remember that the differential between pressures at front and rear is of particular importance in maintaining stability on the road. The recommended differential should be maintained, and where higher pressures are recommended for high speeds or heavy loads, pressures should be tailored to the operating conditions. Check the tires when they are cold in order to ensure accurate pressure measurement. Do not bleed air out of hot tires to maintain the recommended pressure level. Remember to use valve caps to keep dirt out of the valve core.

Tires should be rotated about every 6,000 miles. This will even out wear that might otherwise destroy a small segment of the tread prematurely, thereby wasting the remainder. The spare tire should be included in the rotation, as inactivity is harmful to a tire.

The tires should be statically and dynamically balanced at the first sign of ride roughness. Static balance means that the tire would remain in any selected position without turning itself on the wheel bearings with the vehicle on a lift. Dynamic balance refers to distribution of weight from side to side of the tire. Static balance is performed with the tire at rest; dynamic balance is done with the tire in motion.

Generally, new tires should not be balanced until they have been operated for several hundred miles to ensure a minimal further change in weight distribution in the tire.

Tire Selection

Higher-priced tires do not necessarily increase cost per operating mile. Radial tires offer the longest mileage, and belted bias tires last longer than bias ply designs. The increased manufacturing cost is not usually as great as the gain in mileage.

If possible, all four tires on an automobile should be of the same type. If mixing is necessary, make sure that tires on one axle are not of different designs.

These precautions are particularly important with radial tires, which have vastly different cornering characteristics. If radials and another design *must* be mixed, put the radials on the rear axle.

Rims are generally 5–5½ in wide, with some optional rims, as on station wagons, going as wide as 6 in. Super wide tires sometimes use rims up to 7 in. wide. Generally, it is permissible to go one range wider than original equipment without changing the rims. In other words, an E78 or E70 tire may use a 5½ in. rim with good results. In going to E60 tires, however, wider (7–8 in.) rims are recommended. Tire dealers have charts showing recommended rim widths for various tire sizes.

It should be remembered that, when

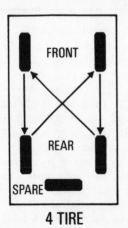

4 TIRE

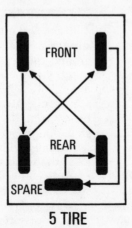

5 TIRE

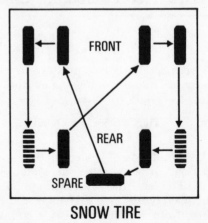

SNOW TIRE

Various methods of tire rotation (Courtesy of Firestone Tire & Rubber Co)

wider rims and tires are used, wheel bearing wear may be increased due to the increased load on the bottom of the outer bearing and the top of the inner bearing.

Tire Size Designation Chart *

The tire industry recently changed its tire size designations from a numerical to a combination alphabetical-numerical system.

For example, it's no longer an 8.25-15. That size is now known as G78-15. Basically, the higher the letter the larger the tire size, as the accompanying chart illustrates. The following numerals show the relationship of tire width to height. The last two numbers show the wheel size.

E78-14	7.35-14
F78-14	7.75-14
G78-14	8.25-14
H78-14	8.55-14
E78-15	7.35-15
G78-15	8.25-15
H78-15	8.55-15
J78-15	8.85-15
L78-15	9.15-15

* Courtesy of Firestone Tire & Rubber Co.

Appendix

General Conversion Table

Multiply by	To convert	To	
2.54	Inches	Centimeters	.3937
30.48	Feet	Centimeters	.0328
.914	Yards	Meters	1.094
1.609	Miles	Kilometers	.621
.645	Square inches	Square cm.	.155
.836	Square yards	Square meters	1.196
16.39	Cubic inches	Cubic cm.	‑.061
28.3	Cubic feet	Liters	.0353
.4536	Pounds	Kilograms	2.2045
4.546	Gallons	Liters	.22
.068	Lbs./sq. in. (psi)	Atmospheres	14.7
.138	Foot pounds	Kg. m.	7.23
1.014	H.P. (DIN)	H.P. (SAE)	.9861
——	To obtain	From	Multiply by

Note: 1 cm. equals 10 mm.; 1 mm. equals .0394″.

Conversion—Common Fractions to Decimals and Millimeters

INCHES			INCHES			INCHES		
Common Fractions	Decimal Fractions	Millimeters (approx.)	Common Fractions	Decimal Fractions	Millimeters (approx.)	Common Fractions	Decimal Fractions	Millimeters (approx.)
1/128	.008	0.20	11/32	.344	8.73	43/64	.672	17.07
1/64	.016	0.40	23/64	.359	9.13	11/16	.688	17.46
1/32	.031	0.79	3/8	.375	9.53	45/64	.703	17.86
3/64	.047	1.19	25/64	.391	9.92	23/32	.719	18.26
1/16	.063	1.59	13/32	.406	10.32	47/64	.734	18.65
5/64	.078	1.98	27/64	.422	10.72	3/4	.750	19.05
3/32	.094	2.38	7/16	.438	11.11	49/64	.766	19.45
7/64	.109	2.78	29/64	.453	11.51	25/32	.781	19.84
1/8	.125	3.18	15/32	.469	11.91	51/64	.797	20.24
9/64	.141	3.57	31/64	.484	12.30	13/16	.813	20.64
5/32	.156	3.97	1/2	.500	12.70	53/64	.828	21.03
11/64	.172	4.37	33/64	.516	13.10	27/32	.844	21.43
3/16	.188	4.76	17/32	.531	13.49	55/64	.859	21.83
13/64	.203	5.16	35/64	.547	13.89	7/8	.875	22.23
7/32	.219	5.56	9/16	.563	14.29	57/64	.891	22.62
15/64	.234	5.95	37/64	.578	14.68	29/32	.906	23.02
1/4	.250	6.35	19/32	.594	15.08	59/64	.922	23.42
17/64	.266	6.75	39/64	.609	15.48	15/16	.938	23.81
9/32	.281	7.14	5/8	.625	15.88	61/64	.953	24.21
19/64	.297	7.54	41/64	.641	16.27	31/32	.969	24.61
5/16	.313	7.94	21/32	.656	16.67	63/64	.984	25.00
21/64	.328	8.33						

Conversion—Millimeters to Decimal Inches

mm	inches	mm	inches	mm	inches	mm	inches	mm	inches
1	.039 370	31	1.220 470	61	2.401 570	91	3.582 670	210	8.267 700
2	.078 740	32	1.259 840	62	2.440 940	92	3.622 040	220	8.661 400
3	.118 110	33	1.299 210	63	2.480 310	93	3.661 410	230	9.055 100
4	.157 480	34	1.338 580	64	2.519 680	94	3.700 780	240	9.448 800
5	.196 850	35	1.377 949	65	2.559 050	95	3.740 150	250	9.842 500
6	.236 220	36	1.417 319	66	2.598 420	96	3.779 520	260	10.236 200
7	.275 590	37	1.456 689	67	2.637 790	97	3.818 890	270	10.629 900
8	.314 960	38	1.496 050	68	2.677 160	98	3.858 260	280	11.032 600
9	.354 330	39	1.535 430	69	2.716 530	99	3.897 630	290	11.417 300
10	.393 700	40	1.574 800	70	2.755 900	100	3.937 000	300	11.811 000
11	.433 070	41	1.614 170	71	2.795 270	105	4.133 848	310	12.204 700
12	.472 440	42	1.653 540	72	2.834 640	110	4.330 700	320	12.598 400
13	.511 810	43	1.692 910	73	2.874 010	115	4.527 550	330	12.992 100
14	.551 180	44	1.732 280	74	2.913 380	120	4.724 400	340	13.385 800
15	.590 550	45	1.771 650	75	2.952 750	125	4.921 250	350	13.779 500
16	.629 920	46	1.811 020	76	2.992 120	130	5.118 100	360	14.173 200
17	.669 290	47	1.850 390	77	3.031 490	135	5.314 950	370	14.566 900
18	.708 660	48	1.889 760	78	3.070 860	140	5.511 800	380	14.960 600
19	.748 030	49	1.929 130	79	3.110 230	145	5.708 650	390	15.354 300
20	.787 400	50	1.968 500	80	3.149 600	150	5.905 500	400	15.748 000
21	.826 770	51	2.007 870	81	3.188 970	155	6.102 350	500	19.685 000
22	.866 140	52	2.047 240	82	3.228 340	160	6.299 200	600	23.622 000
23	.905 510	53	2.086 610	83	3.267 710	165	6.496 050	700	27.559 000
24	.944 880	54	2.125 980	84	3.307 080	170	6.692 900	800	31.496 000
25	.984 250	55	2.165 350	85	3.346 450	175	6.889 750	900	35.433 000
26	1.023 620	56	2.204 720	86	3.385 820	180	7.086 600	1000	39.370 000
27	1.062 990	57	2.244 090	87	3.425 190	185	7.283 450	2000	78.740 000
28	1.102 360	58	2.283 460	88	3.464 560	190	7.480 300	3000	118.110 000
29	1.141 730	59	2.322 830	89	3.503 903	195	7.677 150	4000	157.480 000
30	1.181 100	60	2.362 200	90	3.543 300	200	7.874 000	5000	196.850 000

To change decimal millimeters to decimal inches, position the decimal point where desired on either side of the millimeter measurement shown and reset the inches decimal by the same number of digits in the same direction. For example, to convert .001 mm into decimal inches, reset the decimal behind the 1 mm (shown on the chart) to .001; change the decimal inch equivalent (.039″ shown) to .00039″).

Tap Drill Sizes

	National Fine or S.A.E.			National Coarse or U.S.S.	
Screw & Tap Size	Threads Per Inch	Use Drill Number	Screw & Tap Size	Threads Per Inch	Use Drill Number
No. 5	44	37	No. 5	40	39
No. 6	40	33	No. 6	32	36
No. 8	36	29	No. 8	32	29
No. 10	32	21	No. 10	24	25
No. 12	28	15	No. 12	24	17
1/4	28	3	1/4	20	8
7/16	24	1	5/16	18	F
3/8	24	Q	3/8	16	5/16
7/16	20	W	7/16	14	U
1/2	20	29/64	1/2	13	27/64
9/16	18	33/64	9/16	12	31/64
5/8	18	37/64	5/8	11	17/32
3/4	16	11/16	3/4	10	21/32
7/8	14	13/16	7/8	9	49/64
1 1/8	12	1 3/64	1	8	7/8
1 1/4	12	1 11/64	1 1/8	7	63/64
1 1/2	12	1 27/64	1 1/4	7	1 7/64
			1 1/2	6	1 11/32

Decimal Equivalent Size of the Number Drills

Drill No.	Decimal Equivalent	Drill No.	Decimal Equivalent	Drill No.	Decimal Equivalent
80	.0135	53	.0595	26	.1470
79	.0145	52	.0635	25	.1495
78	.0160	51	.0670	24	.1520
77	.0180	50	.0700	23	.1540
76	.0200	49	.0730	22	.1570
75	.0210	48	.0760	21	.1590
74	.0225	47	.0785	20	.1610
73	.0240	46	.0810	19	.1660
72	.0250	45	.0820	18	.1695
71	.0260	44	.0860	17	.1730
70	.0280	43	.0890	16	.1770
69	.0292	42	.0935	15	.1800
68	.0310	41	.0960	14	.1820
67	.0320	40	.0980	13	.1850
66	.0330	39	.0995	12	.1890
65	.0350	38	.1015	11	.1910
64	.0360	37	.1040	10	.1935
63	.0370	36	.1065	9	.1960
62	.0380	35	.1100	8	.1990
61	.0390	34	.1110	7	.2010
60	.0400	33	.1130	6	.2040
59	.0410	32	.1160	5	.2055
58	.0420	31	.1200	4	.2090
57	.0430	30	.1285	3	.2130
56	.0465	29	.1360	2	.2210
55	.0520	28	.1405	1	.2280
54	.0550	27	.1440		

Decimal Equivalent Size of the Letter Drills

Letter Drill	Decimal Equivalent	Letter Drill	Decimal Equivalent	Letter Drill	Decimal Equivalent
A	.234	J	.277	S	.348
B	.238	K	.281	T	.358
C	.242	L	.290	U	.368
D	.246	M	.295	V	.377
E	.250	N	.302	W	.386
F	.257	O	.316	X	.397
G	.261	P	.323	Y	.404
H	.266	Q	.332	Z	.413
I	.272	R	.339		

ANTI-FREEZE CHART

Temperatures Shown in Degrees Fahrenheit
+32 is Freezing

oling stem pacity uarts	Quarts of ETHYLENE GLYCOL Needed for Protection to Temperatures Shown Below													
	1	2	3	4	5	6	7	8	9	10	11	12	13	14
10	+24°	+16°	+ 4°	−12°	−34°	−62°								
11	+25	+18	+ 8	− 6	−23	−47								
12	+26	+19	+10	0	−15	−34	−57°							
13	+27	+21	+13	+ 3	− 9	−25	−45							
14			+15	+ 6	− 5	−18	−34							
15			+16	+ 8	0	−12	−26							
16			+17	+10	+ 2	− 8	−19	−34	−52°					
17			+18	+12	+ 5	− 4	−14	−27	−42					
18			+19	+14	+ 7	0	−10	−21	−34	−50°				
19			+20	+15	+ 9	+ 2	− 7	−16	−28	−42				
20				+16	+10	+ 4	− 3	−12	−22	−34	−48°			
21				+17	+12	+ 6	0	− 9	−17	−28	−41			
22				+18	+13	+ 8	+ 2	− 6	−14	−23	−34	−47°		
23				+19	+14	+ 9	+ 4	− 3	−10	−19	−29	−40		
24				+19	+15	+10	+ 5	0	− 8	−15	−23	−34	−46°	
25				+20	+16	+12	+ 7	+ 1	− 5	−12	−20	−29	−40	−50°
26					+17	+13	+ 8	+ 3	− 3	− 9	−16	−25	−34	−44
27					+18	+14	+ 9	+ 5	− 1	− 7	−13	−21	−29	−39
28					+18	+15	+10	+ 6	+ 1	− 5	−11	−18	−25	−34
29					+19	+16	+12	+ 7	+ 2	− 3	− 8	−15	−22	−29
30					+20	+17	+13	+ 8	+ 4	− 1	− 6	−12	−18	−25

For capacities over 30 quarts divide true capacity by 3. Find quarts Anti-Freeze for the ⅓ and multiply by 3 for quarts to add.

For capacities under 10 quarts multiply true capacity by 3. Find quarts Anti-Freeze for the tripled volume and divide by 3 for quarts to add.

To Increase the Freezing Protection of Anti-Freeze Solutions Already Installed

Cooling System Capacity Quarts	Number of Quarts of ETHYLENE GLYCOL Anti-Freeze Required to Increase Protection													
	From +20°F. to					From +10°F. to					From 0°F. to			
	0°	−10°	−20°	−30°	−40°	0°	−10°	−20°	−30°	−40°	−10°	−20°	−30°	−40°
10	1¾	2¼	3	3½	3¾	¾	1½	2¼	2¾	3¼	¾	1½	2	2½
12	2	2¾	3½	4	4½	1	1¾	2½	3¼	3¾	1	1¾	2½	3¼
14	2¼	3¼	4	4¾	5½	1¼	2	3	3¾	4½	1	2	3	3½
16	2½	3½	4½	5¼	6	1¼	2½	3½	4¼	5¼	1¼	2¼	3¼	4
18	3	4	5	6	7	1½	2¾	4	5	5¾	1½	2½	3¾	4¾
20	3¼	4½	5¾	6¾	7½	1¾	3	4¼	5½	6½	1½	2¾	4¼	5¼
22	3½	5	6¼	7¼	8¼	1¾	3¼	4¾	6	7¼	1¾	3¼	4½	5½
24	4	5½	7	8	9	2	3½	5	6½	7½	1¾	3½	5	6
26	4¼	6	7½	8¾	10	2	4	5½	7	8¼	2	3¾	5½	6¾
28	4½	6¼	8	9½	10½	2¼	4¼	6	7½	9	2	4	5¾	7¼
30	5	6¾	8½	10	11½	2½	4½	6½	8	9½	2¼	4¼	6¼	7¾

Test radiator solution with proper hydrometer. Determine from the table the number of quarts of solution to be drawn off from a full cooling system and replace with undiluted anti-freeze, to give the desired increased protection. For example, to increase protection of a 22-quart cooling system containing Ethylene Glycol (permanent type) anti-freeze, from +20°F. to −20°F. will require the replacement of 6¼ quarts of solution with undiluted anti-freeze.

WHEN WOULD YOU RATHER DEAL WITH A PROBLEM DRINKER?

AT THE PARTY.

AFTER THE PARTY.

There is only one answer, of course. But there is another question.

Will you deal with a problem drinker

It won't be easy. He's your friend. You don't want to hurt him or insult him. You don't want to lose a friend. But that is just what may happen.

After the party, your friend is potentially a killer. He's speeding and weaving, endangering his life and the lives of others.

Problem drinkers were responsible for 19,000 highway deaths last year. The killed themselves. They killed innocent people.

And they didn't only kill. They crippled and maimed and destroyed lives without actually taking them.

If your friend has a drinking problem there are many ways you can help him. But first you must help him stay alive.

If you are really his friend, don't help him drink. If he has been drinking, don't let him drive.

Drive him yourself. Call a cab. Take his car keys.

Everything you think you can't do, you must do. At the party.

Write Drunk Driver, Box 2345, Rockville, Maryland 20852.

WHEN A PROBLEM DRINKER DRIVE IT'S YOUR PROBLEM.

U.S. DEPARTMENT OF TRANSPORTATION • NATIONAL HIGHWAY TRAFFIC SAFETY ADMINIST